a taste of . . .
CAPE COD

favorite recipes from
Cape Cod's finest restaurants

by Gillian Drake

Published by
SHANK PAINTER PUBLISHING COMPANY
Provincetown, Mass.

Books in the "Taste of" series:

A TASTE OF . . . CAPE COD
A TASTE OF . . . PROVINCETOWN
A TASTE OF . . . NEWPORT

Copies of books in the "Taste of" series
may be ordered from:

Shank Painter Publishing Co.
Box 143, Provincetown, Mass. 02657

order coupons on page 79

First printing May 1983: 5,000
Second printing July 1983: 5,000

"A Taste of . . . Cape Cod"
designed and written by Gillian Drake

Drawings of restaurants by Katherine Bloom

Text and drawings © Gillian Drake, 1983

Many thanks to Linda Canty
for her help in compiling this book.

I.S.B.N. # 0-9609814-2-X

Printed by Shank Painter Printing Company, Provincetown, Mass. 02657

Introduction

Considering its large area, Cape Cod has surprisingly few fine restaurants which cater to cosmopolitan tastes (that is, if one discounts Provincetown, the town at the tip of the Cape which is becoming increasingly well-known for its varied and interesting selection of top-class restaurants). During the research for this book, however, it became obvious that this sad state of affairs is beginning to change, and that new restaurants of high caliber are now being opened on the Cape with heartening frequency.

This book will help you discover these new restaurants and let you know what to expect from them. These days, it can cost a small fortune to find, by trial and error, new restaurants where you can enjoy an excellent meal in congenial surroundings. Although we have done the discovering for you, we have made no attempt to *rate* these restaurants. We certainly liked their food, their style and their philosophy, and so we merely describe each restaurant to you so you can make up your *own* mind about whether it sounds like your kind of place.

Just about every restaurant featured in this book offers something out-of-the-ordinary as well as excellent food . . . it might be the magnificent waterfront setting of The Regatta; the intimate surroundings of a private home at Cielo; the romantic country-inn atmosphere of Sweet Seasons or the Old Manse; Toni-Lee's unique single-menu restaurant; the party-like ambience at the Cranberry Moose; or the funky surroundings at The Arbor . . . we feel all the restaurants are well worth trying, and we're sure you won't be disappointed at any of them. We weren't.

Needless to say, these are not the *only* restaurants on the Cape worth dining at. We are constantly trying out new places (the Cape is a big area to cover!) and will add them to this book each year as we discover restaurants which seem special to us.

Other restaurants which we highly recommend but could not be included in the first edition of this book for various reasons are: Chillingsworth, an elegant French restaurant in Brewster; High Brewster, a delightful country inn also in Brewster; The Mediterranee in North Truro, a well-known gourmet restaurant under new ownership since 1982; and Aesop's Tables in Wellfleet (under new ownership for the 1983 season) which promises to be a good place to visit.

We should point out that many of the recipes appearing in this book are special dishes which some restaurants might serve only occasionally— in other words, don't necessarily expect to find every recipe appearing in this book on the restaurant's menu when you arrive for dinner.

Contents

The Arbor

While the rest of Orleans tries to keep pace with the modernization of Cape Cod, the Arbor restaurant manages to retain a genuine old-fashioned charm and serene atmosphere. Located in the center of Orleans in an old sea captain's home, this unusual restaurant is known for its creative cuisine and its many intimate dining rooms decorated with an impressive collection of Victorian and Edwardian memorabilia.

The Arbor is renowned for its richly-varied menu with a range that seemingly encompasses the entire culinary spectrum, from fresh fish and seafood to steak, fowl, veal and pasta. Many of the menu items are imaginative interpretations of classical dishes, while others are original creations—for instance, you may order Veal Barbara, Veal Mary or Veal Joany as well as the better-known Veal Milanaise, Marsala and Saltimbocca. The menu is so varied it defies detailed description, but certain dishes stand out as worth mentioning . . . Scrod Arthur, in a white wine sauce with oysters, mushrooms and raisins; Baked Shrimp Calcutta, in a mild curry sauce, topped with almonds and coconut; Oysters a l'Arbor, baked in a sour cream and mustard sauce with mushrooms, almonds and white grapes; Sweetbreads a la Maison, sauteed in white wine with ham, topped with mushroom caps and poulette sauce and served on toast points; and Oyster and Scallop Steven, with cheese and leeks in a cream sauce served over spinach noodles (see following recipe). The Arbor also serves more traditional fare, such as Broiled Half Chicken with Rosemary, pan-sauteed Tournedos with sauce du jour, fresh Catch of the Day, and Calf's Liver with Onions and Bacon. Dinner starts off with a selection from the Arbor's extensive salad bar which consists of such items as marinated mushrooms, cooked lentils, sauced chilled pasta, marinated fresh green beans, and sweet red cabbage, and may be preceded by an appetizer from a list that includes Artichokes a l'Arbor (see following recipe), Oysters Rockefeller, Stuffed Mushrooms and Clams Casino. Pasta dishes may be ordered in half portions as an appetizer or side dish, as well as an entree.

The Arbor is owned and managed by Kendall Bowers and Carol Bakunas, who between them have had many years of experience as both chef and restaurant manager plus a degree from the Culinary Institute. Kendall had spent childhood summers on the Cape and decided to settle in Orleans. In 1972 he found the perfect building—an old guest house dating from the 1850s—and set about transforming it into an attractive and unique restaurant. The downstairs rooms were turned into small, intimate dining rooms decorated with what Carol calls "cozy clutter"— old photos and prints, tinware, old lanterns, antique bottles, in fact, anything worth collecting. Tables are covered with flowered tablecloths and set with old floral-patterned china and fresh flowers. One dining room has an open fireplace with brick hearth, old wood paneling and a mass of hanging plants at the windows which overlook a pretty garden; another room contains the bar, as well as a few dining tables, and a velvet-covered couch, a barber's chair and an old school desk clustered around a woodstove provide a cozy corner in which to enjoy a drink before dinner. Even outside, the immaculately-kept lawns and flower beds have been embellished with old farm implements, artifacts and garden ornaments. To complete the country feeling, a small flock of domestic geese stand guard in a pen at the side of the building.

The Binnacle Tavern, a unique bar with a nautical decor and bare floorboards, is adjacent to the restaurant and is open from noon until 1 a.m.

The Arbor is a lovely place to discover, a place where you'll find you can get away from it all and forget the pressures of everyday life in surroundings which take you back to another era.

Arbor Restaurant
Route 28 at Route 6A
Orleans, Mass. 02653
Telephone: 255-4847

Open: seven days a week, year round
Lunch: 12 to 2:30 daily
Dinner: 5 to 10 nightly
Binnacle Tavern: late supper from 9 to 12
                 bar 12 noon to 1 a.m.

Seats: 85
Children's portions: are available
License: full liquor license
Credit cards: AMX, MC, VISA
Parking: ample private parking
Reservations: advised, call 255-4847
In summer: lunch on the patio; dinner on the terrace.

Hot Artichokes a l'Arbor   Serves 2 generously

12 artichoke hearts
1 hard-cooked egg, chopped
½ cup mushrooms, sliced
2 teaspoons capers
4 tablespoons dry vermouth
Butter
Salt and pepper
Chopped parsley

Melt enough butter in a saute pan to cover the bottom of the pan. Gently saute artichokes hearts, egg, mushrooms and capers in butter until mushrooms soften. Season with salt and pepper. Add the vermouth and cook for a further two minutes. Serve hot, garnished with parsley.

Oyster & Scallop Steven   Serves 2

12 oysters and their juice
20 scallops
¼ teaspoon chopped leeks
2 teaspoons grated cheese
2 tablespoons white wine
2 cups white cream sauce
2 cups cooked spinach noodles
Salt and pepper
Butter

Melt enough butter in a saute pan to cover the bottom. Add leeks and shellfish and simmer gently until cooked. Add wine and cheese and season with salt and pepper. Add the cream sauce and heat through.

Add cooked spinach noodles to the pan and toss so noodles are coated. When noodles are heated through, serve on heated plates and garnish with parsley.

Filet of Sole Capri

10 oz. sole filets
1 banana
2 teaspoons white wine
2 teaspoons lemon juice
2 teaspoons water
Flour
Egg wash
Salt and pepper
Chopped parsley

Flour sole and dip in egg wash. Saute sole in a pan in a good grade of oil. Slice banana lengthwise, dip in flour and egg wash, and saute with the sole. Season with salt and pepper to taste.

Sprinkle lemon juice, wine and water around the edges of the pan. Saute fish until it is done. Remove fish and place on a warm platter. Heat pan juices and pour over fish. Sprinkle with chopped parsley.

Lobster Kendall

8 oz. lobster meat
8 oz. scallops
2 teaspoons chopped leeks
½ cup sliced mushrooms
2 teaspoons butter
2 tablespoons port wine
2 cups light cream sauce
1/8 cup dark raisins
Salt and pepper

Lightly saute lobster meat, scallops, leeks, mushrooms and raisins in butter until cooked. Add the port wine and salt and pepper to taste and heat through. Add the cream sauce and simmer. Serve in a casserole garnished with chopped parsley

Chicken Milanaise

Serves 2

2 8-oz. boneless chicken breasts
2 teaspoons lemon juice
2 teaspoons white wine
Salt and pepper
Oil

Batter:

beat together:
4 eggs
4 oz. light cream
2 cloves garlic, finely chopped
2 teaspoons chopped parsley
2 tablespoons grated cheese

Flatten chicken breasts as you would veal and remove the skin. Dip in flour and then in batter. Saute in hot oil on both sides until almost done.

Sprinkle lemon juice, wine and 2 teaspoons water around the edge of pan. Shake pan to mix ingredients and continue to heat until liquid has reduced. Keep warm in oven until ready to serve. Garnish with lemon wedges.

Chocolate Mousse

Serves 4 to 6

6 oz. semi-sweet chocolate chips
3 egg yolks, beaten well
3 egg whites, beaten stiff
½ cup heavy cream, whipped

Melt chocolate in a double boiler. Add beaten egg yolks to chocolate and stir to mix. Gently fold in the egg whites until the mousse is an even color. Fold in the whipped cream. Pipe or spoon into ramekins or parfait glasses. Decorate with whipped cream and chocolate shavings.

Cafe Elizabeth

Cafe Elizabeth is a charming restaurant situated a few blocks from the ocean just off Route 28 in the picturesque town of Harwich Port. Originally a sea captain's home, the building has been turned into a fine restaurant featuring French cuisine, while managing to maintain the flavor of an antique Cape Cod house.

Chef-owner E. Mark Chaput and his wife Betsy have traveled and worked throughout the United States, but eventually realized that they felt most at home on Cape Cod. So they decided to start a new life on the Cape and opened Cafe Elizabeth in June 1982. The word spread quickly and Cafe Elizabeth's reputation for serving fine food in attractive surroundings was soon firmly established.

The menu features classic French dishes, with an emphasis on fresh veal and local seafood. Entrees include Sole Meuniere, Scallops Provencal and Paupiettes de Veaux aux Duxelles Bearnaise (see following recipe); a specialty of the house is Veal Elizabeth—a creation of the chef, this dish combines mushrooms, shallots and crabmeat in a white wine and cream sauce. Hors d'oeuvres include Escargots en Croute (snails baked in garlic butter and served with puff pastry), Terrine de Coquilles St. Jacques a la Creme (chilled scallop mousse garnished with a herb cream sauce), and Canard aux Dijonaise Froid (sliced duck with a mustard vinaigrette). All the food, including soups, sauces, desserts and breads, is made on the premises.

Throughout the summer, Cafe Elizabeth serves chilled soups and desserts that take advantage of seasonal vegetables and fruits—these summer specialties might include Summer Fruit Trifle, or a Lemon Mousse Charlotte with a fresh strawberry sauce. A particularly delicious dessert served here is Creme Brulee (see following recipe) . . . literally "burnt cream", this rich custard of cream and egg yolks is covered with a layer of brown sugar and placed under a broiler until the sugar melts into crisp caramel—a sinful dessert indeed!

The entrance to Cafe Elizabeth is bordered by colorful flower beds and hanging plants. Inside, the dining room, which seats 65, is elegant and attracive, with crisp linen, fresh flowers and candles on the tables. Hand-colored French prints and floral watercolors adorn the walls, and flowered drapes and potted plants complete the decor. Off the main dining room is an enclosed porch where a few tables have a distant view of Vineyard Sound.

Separate from the dining room is the Cafe Lounge, where the atmosphere is more informal. The rustic decor is accented with print tablecloths, exposed beams and baskets of dried flowers. A separate menu is served in the Cafe Lounge consisting of salads, soups, desserts and lighter fare. A meal in the lounge might consist of a fresh lobster with avocado salad; or a selection of fruit, cheeses and homemade bread might serve as an early supper or a late snack. Cafe Elizabeth has a full liquor license and a carefully-chosen wine list featuring French and Californian wines.

Mark and Betsy Chaput are totally dedicated to the restaurant business; their aim is to serve a few people extremely well . . . to devote personal attention to both the food preparation and the service for each individual customer. They feel they have at last found a home on Cape Cod and their happiness in finding a location as lovely as Harwich Port and the pleasure they take in the successful running of their restaurant seems to permeate every aspect of their business.

Cafe Elizabeth
31 Sea Street
Harwich Port, Mass. 02646
Telephone: 432-1147

Open: seven days a week, in-season
Closed: Monday & Tuesday, off-season
Dinner: 6 to 10
Brunch: 11 to 2
Seats: 65
Children's portions: not available
License: full liquor license
Credit cards: MC & VISA
Parking: plenty of private parking
Reservations: advised, call 432-1147

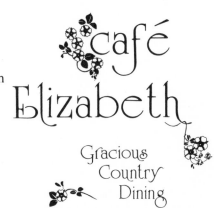

café
Elizabeth
Gracious
Country
Dining

Vinaigrette Salad Dressing

Serves 6

2 tablespoons wine vinegar
1 tablespoon lemon juice
¼ teaspoon salt
½ teaspoon Dijon mustard
8 tablespoons olive oil
1 teaspoon freshly ground black pepper
1 teaspoon minced shallots
1 teaspoon minced garlic
Optional: fresh herbs such as basil, chives and parsley

Blend all ingredients well together or shake in a jar.

Paupiettes de Veau aux Duxelles, Sauce Bearnaise

Serves 4

1½ lbs. veal, cut from the leg in 8 slices
4 eggs
1 tablespoon milk
Flour for dredging
8 tablespoons clarified butter
1½ cups duxelles
Juice of 1 lemon
Dry white wine to taste
Salt and pepper
1½ cups sauce Bearnaise

Prepare duxelles and sauce Bearnaise (recipes follow). Preheat oven to 350 degrees. Place veal slices between waxed paper and pound thin with a flat mallet. Season with salt and pepper. Combine eggs and milk in a shallow bowl. Dredge veal slices in flour, then dip them in egg batter. Heat butter in a large skillet (more than one skillet may be needed, in which case more butter may be required). Quickly saute egg-coated veal slices in hot (but not browned) butter until golden on both sides. Transfer veal slices to a work surface. Place a spoonful of duxelles at one end of each veal slice and roll it up. Secure with a toothpick. Return veal slices to the skillet and add lemon juice and white wine to taste. Bake in oven for 10 or 15 minutes or until heated through.

Remove toothpicks and transfer Veal Paupiettes to a warmed serving platter. Top with sauce Bearnaise.

Duxelles:

1 medium onion, diced finely
1 tablespoon minced garlic
½ lb. mushrooms, diced finely
1 tablespoon chopped parsley
1 tablespoon chopped chives
1 tablespoon ground nutmeg
1 tablespoon crumbled dried thyme
1 tablespoon each port wine,
**   brandy and dry white wine**
5 tablespoons clarified butter
2 tablespoons unflavored breadcrumbs

Saute onions and garlic in butter in a 10 or 12 inch skillet until tender. Add the rest of the ingredients and cook until most of the moisture is absorbed. Remove from heat and combine breadcrumbs thoroughly. Refrigerate in a covered container.

Sauce Bearnaise

3 tablespoons tarragon vinegar
1 tablespoon chopped tarragon leaves
3 tablespoons dry white wine
1 teaspoon each of chopped parsley, chervil
**   and minced shallots**
1 teaspoon Worcestershire Sauce
3 egg yolks
¾ cup melted butter
Salt and pepper

In a small saucepan combine all ingredients except eggs, butter, salt and pepper. Cook over moderate heat and reduce to ⅓ cup liquid. Let cool briefly. Transfer to double boiler over hot, not boiling, water. Add egg yolks and whisk until mixture is hot and creamy. Add melted butter slowly, mixing thoroughly. Remove sauce from heat, season with salt and pepper to taste and keep warm until ready to serve.

Honey-Glazed Carrots with Dill

Serves 4

1 lb. fresh carrots
1 cup honey
1 tablespoon fresh dill
1 tablespoon fresh parsley
1 tablespoon chopped scallions
2 tablespoons butter
Salt and pepper to taste

Scrape carrots and cut into sticks 2" long by ¼" wide. Par-boil carrots. Strain in colander. Melt butter in a skillet, add carrots and rest of ingredients. Saute until heated through and serve.

Creme Brulee

Serves 6 to 8

3 cups heavy cream
⅓ cup sugar
6 egg yolks
2 teaspoons vanilla essence
Brown sugar

Preheat oven to 300 degrees. Bring cream to scalding point in the top of a double boiler. Add sugar, stirring constantly.

In another bowl whip egg yolks with vanilla essence. Pour hot cream over the egg yolks, stirring mixture as you pour. Pour the egg custard into a baking dish set inside a large pan filled part way with warm water. Bake in oven until knife inserted comes out clean. Refrigerate until cool.

Sprinkle with brown sugar and place under broiler until sugar has melted and caramelized. Serve in individual glasses garnished with whipped cream and shredded lemon rind.

Chanterelle

Chanterelle is tucked away in the back of a small shopping center off Route 6A in Yarmouthport, and unless you knew of its existence, it's not likely you would stumble upon it. Since opening in June, 1981, Chanterelle has won a good following devoted to its imaginative approach and high level of finesse. Serving basically a Gallic menu with a strong bias towards Nouvelle Cuisine, Chanterelle produces dishes with refinement and a lightness of touch only possible when first-class ingredients are used.

The restaurant gets it name from one of the rarest and most distinctive varieties of wild mushroom. A native of France and Switzerland, they are egg-yellow and firm, with a fragrance of apricots and a slightly peppery but agreeable flavor. Their restaurant was so named by owners Bert Kennison, Kathy Cronin-Kennison, Paul Casey and Lester Allen III because of this wild mushroom's unique but delectable flavor combined with its rarity. They feel their restaurant is unqiue because the owners have equal shares in the business and are dedicated to growth through sharing. They all have had extensive experience in creative cuisine as executive chefs, maitre d's and general managers and consequently bring a great deal of expertise and a good level of sophistication to their business.

The menu at Chanterelle is small but interesting and changes four or five times a year to take advantage of seasonal items, such as local fresh fish, fruit and vegetables. This menu is augmented by daily specials, which might include Veal Chanterelle (see following recipe); Veal Paupiette—stuffed with boursin cheese and smoked salmon, with lime vermouth beurre blanc; Chicken en Papillote—baked in parchment paper with prosciutto, fresh mushrooms, fontina cheese and an herb compound

---

butter; Fillet of Fish in Phyllo—baked in pastry with a fennel mirepoix and tomato-saffron sauce; Sole with Zucchini and Melon, poached in white wine with a light curry sauce; Swordfish Dijonaise—marinated in a mustard sauce, sauteed with white wine, morels, coulis of fresh tomatoes and basil; Roast Duckling with a choice of bigarade or cranberry caraway sauce; and Rack of Lamb Chanterelle, roasted with anise seed and sweet garlic. The selection of soups and appetizers changes almost daily—an evening soup special and a fish soup du jour are both offered, and special appetizers often appearing on the menu include Oysters a la Moutarde (Chanterelle won a Cape Cod Seafood Council award for this creation—see following recipe); Moules Mariniere; Quiche du Jour; or maybe Fresh Artichoke stuffed with lobster. A house salad of romaine and red leaf lettuce accompanies dinner—this year a house dressing of creme fraiche, raspberry vinegar and dill is offered with salads. Recently, a luncheon gourmet salad bar has been introduced in the lounge area—this is converted to a chilled appetizer/raw bar in the evenings.

There are two small dining rooms at the Chanterelle, each seating about 30 guests. For lunch, bare tables are set with attractive napkins and table mats, while for dinner a proliferation of white linen creates a more sophisticated atmosphere and candles in clear glass bowls provide soft, romantic lighting. Plain white walls are hung with a changing display of art work, mostly on consignment. A large bow window in one of the dining rooms overlooks the attractive Italian-style courtyard garden around which the small complex of shops is built.

Chanterelle has recently been awarded three-star status by the restaurant critics of both the Boston Globe and the Boston Herald American—opinions that affirm many people's belief that Chanterelle is a delightful restaurant which lives up to its reputation for serving fine food at affordable prices. (For those who haven't discovered Chanterelle yet . . . it's located a quarter of a mile west of Union Street—exit 8 of Mid-Cape Highway/Route 6—on the south side of Route 6A.)

Chanterelle
411 Main Street
Yarmouthport
Telephone: 362-8195

Open: seven days a week, all year
Lunch: 11:30 to 2:30
Dinner: 5:30 to 10:00
Seats: 65
License: full liquor license
Credit Cards: AMEX, MC, VISA
Parking: large parking lot
Reservations: advised, call 362-8195

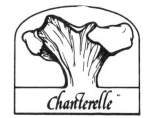

Chanterelle Restaurant and Lounge Dedicated to Fine Food

Oyster Saffron Stew

Serves 6

This recipe won an award from the Cape Cod Seafood Council.

18 oysters, shucked and cleaned
   (reserve liquid)
3 tablespoons butter
1 quart fish stock (clam juice
   may be substituted)
1 large baking potato, peeled and diced
1 large carrot, chopped
1 large stalk celery, chopped
1 medium onion, chopped
1 lemon, halved
1 teaspoon dried saffron thread
   or powdered saffron
2 tablespoons fresh dill, chopped or
   one teaspoon dried dillweed
½ cup heavy cream

Melt butter in a large saucepan. Add carrot, celery and onion. Saute over moderate heat for 10 minutes. Add fish stock, reserved oyster liquid, potato, lemon half, saffron and fresh dill. Simmer for 20 minutes or until potatoes are tender. Puree mixture in a blender or food processor. Reheat gently and add heavy cream and oysters. Stew is ready when oysters begin to curl. Season with salt and white pepper. Ladle into bowls and garnish with thinly sliced lemon and a sprig of dill.

Oysters Moutarde

Serves 6

This recipe won an award from the Cape Cod Seafood Council.

18 oysters, shucked
   (reserve and clean shells)
1 12 oz. bottle beer
1½ cups all-purpose flour
1 tablespoon paprika
½ teaspoon dry mustard
Pinch salt

In a glass bowl combine the beer, paprika, baking powder, salt and mustard. Stir with a wire whisk until smooth. Coat each oyster in this batter and deep-fry at 350 degrees for approximately 1½ minutes or until batter is crisp. Drain and pat with paper towels. Serve immediately—spoon sauce into reserved oyster shells and top each with a fried oyster. Garnish with fresh chopped parsley.

Mustard Sauce

3 cups heavy cream
½ cup dry white wine
¼ cup Dijon mustard
1 small bay leaf
Juice of ½ lemon
1 tablespoon fresh parsley, chopped

Combine cream, mustard, wine, bay leaf and lemon juice in a medium saucepan and simmer over moderate heat. Reduce mixture until 1½ cups remain. Season with salt and pepper.

Veal Chanterelle

Serves 4

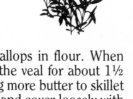

1½ lb. veal scallopine, pounded to ¼" thickness
4 tablespoons butter
2 tablespoons shallots, finely chopped
1 7—8 oz. can chanterelles, drained
1 cup fresh mushrooms, thinly sliced
2 tablespoons Cognac
2 tablespoons apricot liqueur
½ cup demi-glace
½ cup heavy cream

Melt the butter in a 12" skillet. Dredge veal scallops in flour. When butter is about to turn brown, saute one half of the veal for about 1½ minutes per side. Saute the rest of the veal, adding more butter to skillet as needed. Remove veal from the pan to a platter and cover loosely with foil to keep warm.

Pour off the fat from the pan. Add the shallots, fresh mushrooms and chanterelles and saute for about 15 seconds over medium-high heat. Remove pan and add the Cognac and apricot liqueur. Return the pan to the heat and cook for an additional 30 seconds. Add the demi-glace and reduce the sauce by half. Add heavy cream and cook down until the sauce is thick enough to coat the veal. Add salt and white pepper to taste. Pour sauce over veal and serve immediately.

Frozen Mocha Mousse with
Bailey's Irish Cream Chocolate Sauce
Serves 6

Mocha Ice Cream—makes 1 quart

8 large egg whites
½ cup granulated sugar
1 tablespoon white vinegar
1 cup heavy cream
2 teaspoons instant coffee diluted in
**   1 tablespoon warm water**

Combine the egg whites and sugar in a food processor fitted with the metal blade. Process for 8 seconds. With the machine running, add the vinegar and process for 2 to 2½ minutes or until the egg whites are stiff but not dry. Transfer the egg whites to a separate bowl, but do not clean the work bowl. Add heavy cream to processor bowl and process for 20 to 25 seconds. Add the coffee mixture and pulse once. Place the beaten egg whites in a ring on top of the whipped cream in the processor. Pulse 2 or 3 times or until almost all the egg whites are incorporated. Place in a container and freeze for 3 hours or until firm.

Bailey's Irish Cream Chocolate Sauce—makes 1½ cups

8 oz. semi-sweet chocolate chips
1 cup heavy cream
1 tablespoon instant espresso coffee diluted in ¼ cup warm water
¾ cup Bailey's Irish Cream
Confectioners sugar to taste

Melt chocolate in a double boiler. Add diluted espresso coffee. Mix well. Add heavy cream and Bailey's Irish Cream. Serve over mocha frozen mousse.

Cielo

Dining at Cielo is like joining a dinner party at a friend's house—and that's exactly what this restaurant is, a private home and art gallery where one can have lunch or dinner prepared personally by the owners. Self-trained cooks Richard Polak and Hayes Black had always been told by friends that they cooked so well they should open a restaurant, and they finally decided to do just that in the 100-year-old Cape salt box where they now live in Wellfleet. The house is located on one of the loveliest salt marshes on the Cape and the dining focal point is a deck overlooking the marsh affording a view of the famous Wellfleet landmark of Uncle Tim's Bridge. The Cielo art gallery also doubles as a dining room and here dinner is served amidst a setting of fine art, brilliant art glass and decorative porcelain. Because Cielo is small, the hosts try to separate diners in different areas to afford the most privacy and comfort. Special parties are also accommodated in the living room which Richard and Hayes have decorated in exquisite taste with striking wallpaper, antique furniture and their personal art collection.

The format for dining at Cielo is different from the average restaurant in that there is no menu choice; instead, a single fixed-price menu is devised for each day—these change daily to allow for the greatest creativity in meal planning. Given enough notice, the chefs will also prepare a dinner or luncheon according to a guest's specifications.

A three-course luncheon and a five-course dinner are offered at Cielo. A great deal of thought and time are spent devising the menus for these meals so that they are pleasing and well balanced. As an artist, Richard feels that the "design" of a meal should be as aesthetic as that of a good painting. Therefore, great care is taken in considering colors and textures of food as well as taste to make the overall presentation as satisfying to the senses as possible. At lunch the menu revolves around soups, special salads, pasta dishes, pates, filled crepes, quiches and desserts. The cuisine draws from many ethnic origins as well as more traditional French cooking. One day there may be a middle-European cold fruit soup or Greek avgolemeno, or a dish of cold Szechuan soy noodles with shrimp. Layered terrines combining meat or seafood pates are another speciality. Cielo also has a reputation for fabulous homemade desserts, including a range of fresh fruit mousses and open fruit and custard tartes, as well as specialties such as Sacher Torte, Crepes Bananas Foster, Praline Cheesecake, and Walnut Pound Cake with Butterscotch Frosting (recipes follow for the last two items).

Dinner, served in one sitting at 8 o'clock, is a meal to be savored over several hours. Candlelit tables are set with flowered cloths, fine napery and china and adorned with a miniature flower arrangement fresh from the garden. An appetizer begins the meal, perhaps mussels poached in wine with mustard mayonnaise, a strudel of meat or chicken pate or a seafood crepe. This is followed by a soup or pasta course, and then comes the entree, which might be a Timbale of Sole with Seafood or Salmon Mousse, a Kouliabiac of fresh, poached salmon combined with rice, mushrooms, spinach, artichokes and hard-boiled eggs encased in a philo crust, or loin of pork with sausage stuffing and a fresh sauce of Italian prune plums. A salad follows the entree, and coffee or tea is served with dessert. Guests are encouraged to bring their own wine which the hosts will serve for them as Cielo has no liquor license.

Dining at Cielo is a very special experience—since both Hayes and Richard previously worked in human service professions, they have turned their concern for people to serving their customers and making them feel special. They personally take care of all aspects of the business, from choosing the artwork which fills the gallery to shopping for and preparing the food, to serving the guests who visit their restaurant. Individual attention to detail and aesthetics are both of paramount importance at Cielo, and beauty and imagination as well as quality are strived for at all times.

Cielo
East Main Street
Wellfleet, Mass. 02667
Telephone: 349-2108

Open: May through October
Lunch: by reservation only
Dinner: one seating at 8 p.m., by reservation only
Seats: 16 to 20
Children's portions: not served
License: no liquor license, bring your own
Credit Cards: not accepted—personal checks accepted
Parking: ample parking
Reservations: necessary, call 349-2108

Zucchini Stracciatelle
Italian-style Egg Drop Soup with Zucchini

Serves 8

1 lb. zucchini
2 medium onions
2 or 3 cloves garlic, crushed
Olive oil
2 quarts chicken stock or canned broth
3 eggs
Salt and pepper to taste

Place enough olive oil in a large covered skillet to cover the bottom. Grate the onions and saute in oil with the crushed garlic until onion is wilted. Grate the zucchini and add to the onions. Cover the skillet and saute the mixture until the zucchini releases its liquor.

Meanwhile in a large pot bring the chicken broth to a boil. Lightly beat the eggs and drop the beaten egg mixture in very small batches into the hot broth, stirring constantly. Reduce the heat and spoon the zucchini mixture into the soup until it is thoroughly blended. Season to taste.

Curried Corn & Oyster Chowder

Serves 8

1 pint shucked oysters—reserve liquor
¼ cup butter
¼ cup flour
¼ cup sherry
2 cans (16 oz.) creamed corn
1 can (46 oz.) chicken broth, or
**   preferably, fish stock**
1 cup heavy cream
Curry powder, soy sauce, Tabasco
**   and sugar to taste**

Melt butter in a large, heavy pot. Mix in dry ingredients to form a roux. Add sherry and liquid seasonings to taste, blending them in well. Mix in corn and stir to remove any lumps. Add broth slowly, mixing soup well with each addition. Add cream and heat thoroughly. Add oysters with their liquor and heat through.

Plum Soup

2 cans (30 oz.) plums
¼ cup Amaretto
¼ cup sherry
½ teaspoon cinnamon
½ teaspoon nutmeg
1 quart fruit stock, made by boiling peach
    skins and pits, orange rind and sugar in water

Pit plums and add with liquid from can to blender container. Add last 4 ingredients and fill container with stock. Blend. Combine with any remaining stock and mix well. Serve hot.

Curried Chicken with Apples

Serves 8

4 whole chicken breasts, boned and split
¾ cup butter
2 large onions, chopped
2 cloves garlic, crushed
4 tart, firm apples
3 teaspoons curry powder
½ teaspoon cardamom (seeds or crushed)
½ cup flour
1 to 2 cups chicken broth
¼ cup dry white wine
¼ cup light cream
¼ cup mango chutney, chopped
Salt and pepper to taste

Cut chicken into pieces. Season flour with salt and pepper. Dredge chicken in flour. Reserve flour. In a large skillet, melt ¼ cup butter and saute chicken pieces until they are lightly browned. Remove from pan and keep warm. Reserve pan to make sauce.

In another skillet melt ¼ cup butter and saute the onions and crushed garlic until they are golden. Core and slice apples thin (the skins may be pared or left on depending on your taste). Saute apple slices lightly with the onions. Set aside.

In the original skillet, melt remaining ¼ cup of butter and stir in flour left from dredging chicken to form a roux. Add curry powder, cardamom and the wine. Whisk in the chicken broth to make a smooth sauce. Add the cream and chutney and stir until they are incorporated. Add the chicken and apple mixture and heat through. Serve over saffron rice.

Praline Cheesecake   Serves 8 to 12

1 cup Graham Cracker crumbs and finely-chopped pecans
3 tablespoons sugar
3 tablespoons butter, melted
8 oz. cream cheese
16 oz. Ricotta cheese
1¼ cups packed light brown sugar
2 tablespoons flour
3 eggs, separated
2 teaspoons praline liqueur (or vanilla)
½ cup ground pecans

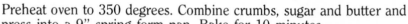

Preheat oven to 350 degrees. Combine crumbs, sugar and butter and press into a 9" spring form pan. Bake for 10 minutes
Combine cheese, sugar and flour and mix well. Add egg yolks, one at a time, mixing in well. Blend in liqueur and chopped nuts. Fold mixture into beaten egg whites and pour into pan on top of crust. Bake in a slow oven at 250 degrees for 1 or 2 hours until set. You may decorate cheesecake with cream whipped with a little sugar and praline liqueur.

Butterscotch-Walnut Pound Cake

3 cups unsifted all-purpose flour
½ teaspoon baking powder
1 cup butter
½ cup shortening
1 lb. light brown sugar
½ lb. granulated sugar
5 eggs
1 teaspoon vanilla extract
1 cup milk
1 cup chopped walnuts

Preheat oven to 350 degrees. Sift the flour and baking powder together. Mix together the butter, shortening and the sugar and beat until fluffy. Add eggs, beating in one at a time. Divide dry ingredients in 4 and beat them in, a quarter at a time, alternating with the milk. Stir in 1 cup chopped walnuts. Bake for 1 to 1½ hours in a greased tube pan.

Frosting:

½ cup butter
1 cup packed light brown sugar
⅓ cup cream or Half & Half
1¼ cups confectioners sugar
1 teaspoon vanilla extract
1 cup walnut halves

Melt butter in a pan. Remove from heat and stir in brown sugar until smooth, reheating to mix. Bring to a boil and boil for 1 minute. Remove from heat and add cream. Slowly bring mixture to a boil. Cool to lukewarm and beat in the confectioners sugar and vanilla extract with a spoon. Add more sugar if the icing is too thin. Spread icing on cake and decorate with walnut halves.

Bananas Flambe Cielo   Serves 2 to 4

---

2 ripe but firm bananas
2 to 3 tablespoons butter
⅓ cup sugar
1 oz. rum
1 oz. coffee brandy
1 oz. banana liqueur
Additional rum to taste

Melt butter in a heavy skillet. Add sugar and heat until sugar melts and starts to brown. Be careful not to let sugar burn, and if mixture becomes too sticky wash down with a little cold water. Slice bananas into the sugar mixture and add the rum and liqueurs. Stir gently but constantly to form a syrup and cook bananas slightly. If the mixture is too thick, add more rum. When serving, heat a little rum, ignite and flambe the sauce.

We serve this sauce over crepes filled with vanilla ice cream for a spectacular and very rich dessert.

Cranberry Moose

From the moment the valet parks your car and the hostess whisks away your coat, you'll know you are in for a pampered evening at the Cranberry Moose. This restaurant is fun, friendly and first-rate, and not in the least pretentious.

Located on Route 6A (Main Street), Yarmouthport, in a building which dates from 1755, the Cranberry Moose was previously known as the Cranberry *Goose*. The owners, by changing only one letter, came up with a witty new name that perfectly reflects their flamboyant approach to the restaurant business.

Owners Jerry Finegold and Tom Rowlands took over this former inn in April 1981 and have livened up the interior of the old building with flair, imagination and excellent taste. Cranberry, naturally, dominates the color scheme, with table linens and accessories as well as the occasional wall in this hue. One of the waiters confessed that the owners are apt to repaint and redecorate any of the three dining rooms whenever the whim takes them. A changing display of art work decorates the restaurant—Jerry and Tom's eclectic taste results in ultra-modern paintings and sculpture hanging side-by-side with antique prints. Each room features a lavish arrangement of exotic fresh flowers, an extravagance designed to add to the festive atmosphere and lift the spirits on even the most dreary of Cape Cod winter days.

At first glance, the menu seems somewhat limited—it merely lists Beef, Fish, Lamb, Veal, Chicken and Duck, plus a variety of appetizers and desserts. However, different variations of each entree is frequently offered, so there's always something interesting and unexpected on the menu. On a recent visit, the beef dish was Tournedos; the veal a delicious cream and mushroom concoction; the fish was fresh salmon; and the duck was boned, lightly roasted and carved into exquisite pink medallions arranged carefully around the plate and garnished with crisp, fresh asparagus. There are also special appetizers, entrees and desserts offered each evening—on this occasion, the special appetizer was Seafood en Croute, a delightful blend of mussels and scallops in a cream sauce served with light puff pastry. All the bread is made on the premises—thinly-sliced toasted white bread with sweet butter precedes dinner, and freshly-baked wholewheat dinner rolls come with the main course. You'll be tempted by the dessert list, no matter how much you may have consumed during the meal—the list changes frequently but might include Fresh Fruits in a Zabione Sauce; a chocolate-coated cream filled puff; Marjolaine—a meringue made with ground walnuts and filled with orange butter cream; Chocolate Mario, a rich cake made with no flour (recipes follow for last two items); and the famous Cranberry Mousse . . . and to round off the meal, guests are presented with a homemade chocolate truffle with their coffee or tea.

The service at the Cranberry Moose is impeccable—friendly, knowledgeable and courteous—and the morale is so high among the staff that they seem to enjoy themselves during the course of the evening as much as the guests. Smartly dressed in cranberry-colored aprons and ties, their self-confidence stems from the knowledge that they are backed by a flawless organization and a top-rate kitchen.

Jerry and Tom describe the atmosphere in their restaurant as "fine food, flowers and friends" and guests will find that spending an evening at the Cranberry Moose is like joining a private party, such is the obvious pleasure the staff and management take in providing a dining experience that is fun as well as being first class.

Cranberry Moose
43 Main Street
Yarmouthport, Mass. 02675
Telephone: 362-3501

Open: year round; seven days a week in season,
open Friday, Saturday and Sunday only off-season.
Dinner: 6 to 9 p.m.
Seats: 75
Children's portions: not available
License: full liquor license
Credit cards: all major cards accepted
Parking: valet parking
Reservations: advised, call 362-3501

Shellfish Bisque

Serves 16

1 tablespoon vinegar
2 cups white wine
2 cups mussel juice
4 shallots, chopped
½ onion, chopped
½ cup chopped tomatoes
½ gallon heavy cream
1 tablespoon tomato paste
Mussels, scallops and/or oysters
Tarragon, bay leaf, thyme, parsley stems
Shrimp shells

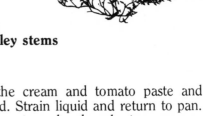

Combine all ingredients except the cream and tomato paste and simmer. Reduce to 2 cups of liquid. Strain liquid and return to pan. Add the heavy cream and tomato paste and reduce by two cups, or until mixture reaches the desired consistency. Garnish with freshly-opened shellfish.

Lobster Bisque:

Follow the same procedure as above, replacing the mussel juice with lobster stock and shrimp shells with lobster carcasses. Garnish with lobster meat, cognac, cream and fresh tarragon.

Smoked Bluefish Pate

Serves 4—6

1 onion
2 shallots
1 lb. smoked bluefish
1 lb. butter
10 oz. cream cheese
Anchovy paste
Lime juice
Cognac
Salt & pepper

Place onion, shallots and bluefish in a blender or food processor and blend until smooth. Add cream cheese and butter and blend in. Add other ingredients to taste. Spoon mixture into pate dish or oblong serving dish and refrigerate until ready to serve. Serve with toast points.

Rack of Lamb   Serves 6

One rack of lamb
¼ cup Dijon mustard
½ teaspoon basil
¼ teaspoon rosemary
2 tablespoons olive oil
1 shallot, chopped
1 clove garlic, chopped
¼ cup fresh bread crumbs
2 tablespoons parsley, or other fresh herbs to taste

Trim rack of lamb. Mix mustard, basil, rosemary and olive oil and brush lamb with the marinade. Let marinate for several hours.

Roast lamb in a very hot oven until cooked to desired degree. Saute chopped shallot in butter; add the chopped garlic, fresh bread crumbs and parsley or herbs and cook gently. Top lamb with this crumb mixture and broil.

Chocolate Mario   Serves 6

10 oz. semi-sweet chocolate
5 oz. butter
8 eggs, separated
1 cup sugar
Triple sec to taste

Melt chocolate and butter together. Mix together the egg yolks and sugar until pale. Add the melted chocolate and butter mixture and stir in. Beat the egg whites until they form stiff peaks. Gently fold the egg whites into the chocolate mixture. Spoon mixture into two 9" x 3½" pans with removable bottoms and bake for 2½ or 3 hours at 250 degrees.

Marjolaine

¾ **cup walnuts**
½ **cup sugar**
1 tablespoon cornstarch
8 eggs (at room temperature)

Preheat oven to 300 degrees. Place a well-oiled (use salad oil) sheet of parchment paper on a baking sheet. Set aside.

Toast the walnuts until well-browned. Grind finely and cool completely. Combine nuts with the sugar and cornstarch and set aside.

Separate eggs and set yolks aside. Whip whites until stiff peaks form. Gently but quickly fold the nuts into the whites. When the nuts are evenly distributed throughout, spread the meringue on the oiled parchment paper in an even layer, forming a rectangle. Place in oven and bake until golden brown. Remove meringue from oven, and, working quickly, peel off the paper and cut meringue into three even squares or rectangles. Handle very gently. Cool on a rack.

Prepare orange butter cream icing and cover two layers with icing ¼" to ½" thick. Place the three layers one on top of each other and ice the top layer. Refrigerate until the icing is firm. Trim the edges and sprinkle the top with confectioner's sugar.

Orange Butter Cream Icing:

6 egg yolks
1 cup confectioner's 10X sugar
½ **cup orange juice concentrate**
1½ **lbs. soft butter, whipped until soft and light**

Combine the egg yolks and sugar in a stainless steel bowl and place bowl in a water bath over heat. (Water should just bubble, not be boiling.) Whisk the mixture until it is light yellow in color and light and airy in texture. Set aside and cool.

Whip in orange flavoring with an electric beater. Whip in the butter, a large tablespoon at a time, making sure it is well incorporated before adding the next tablespoon. Whip in additional flavoring, if desired.

Dom's

For lovers of fine Italian food, Dom's is a real find. It is elegant but unpretentious, professional yet friendly, and the food is superb. Dom's was founded by Dom Caposella, a practicing attorney, who ran a successful restaurant in Boston for many years under the same name. He closed the Boston restaurant in 1979 so he could spend more time on the Cape and soon after, with help from his family, he opened Dom's in Hyannis. Dom recently opened another Dom's in Boston, in Bartlett Place in the North End, so the Hyannis restaurant is now managed by his son Dom Jr., Georgette Silva and a young energetic staff who faithfully follow Dom's guidelines for running a successful and professional restaurant.

Dom's wife, Toni-Lee, who is an expert cook and also the owner of a nearby restaurant which bears her name, has chosen all the recipes for Dom's. She and her family have traveled to Italy to track down their favorite versions of classical Italian dishes so they can present them, unadulterated, in their restaurant. Some of these dishes may be unfamiliar to those who are more used to the robust nature of Southern Italian cooking; at Dom's, where the emphasis in on Northern Italian cuisine, they will find a lightness to the food and a subtlety in the blending of flavors that is only possible when all ingredients are fresh and the dishes cooked to order.

The dining room has a distinct Continental air—it is small, with maybe a dozen tables set with white linen and a single red rose on each. Colorful framed art nouveau posters decorate the walls, and brass wall sconces provide that elusive but desirable quality in a restaurant—perfect lighting. The setting is comfortable and unobtrusive and gives the impression that, here, the food is the star of the show.

Manager Georgette Silva explains that everyone who works at Dom's is trained to cook the many special dishes, so there is no chef as such. Absolutely everything, except the anchovies and maybe tomatoes in the off-season, is fresh and prepared daily, including the pasta. The kitchen is small and functional and is open to the dining room, so diners may see their dishes being prepared to order in heavy pans over open gas flames—no microwave oven in *this* kitchen.

By other standards, Dom's menu might be considered limited; but here, where the flavors of each dish are so distinctly different, there is plenty to choose from. For appetizers, there is Cold Stuffed Eggplant, Clams Casino, Crostini, and Cold Seafood Salad (see following recipe), plus the evening's special—on a recent visit to Dom's this was a Red Clam Soup, a delicious broth of tomato, garlic, carrot, celery, onion and parsley brimming with freshly-shucked littleneck clams.

Homemade pasta, either tagliatelle (wide noodles) or vermicelli (very thin spaghetti), is available with different sauces and may be ordered in half or full portions. Pasta lovers are encouraged to order three or more half portions as a main course, sampling a different sauce with each order; a half portion of pasta may also be ordered as an appetizer. Especially good are the Carbonara sauce, rich and creamy and garnished with pancetta and walnuts (see following recipe), and the Spaghetti con Vongole, delicately flavored with chopped scallions and freshly-shucked littleneck clams, a dish which seems to hint at a Chinese heritage.

A specialty of the house is the prime milk-fed veal dishes, available in eight different preparations from the familiar Marsala, Parmesan and Limone to Cacciatore, Romana and Sienese (with a wild mushroom sauce). All the veal dishes may also be ordered with boned chicken breasts cut into Italian-style scallops substituted for the veal. Other entrees include stuffed pasta dishes and fresh seafood; Lobster Diavolo, Jumbo Shrimp with garlic butter, and pan-fried Prime Steak Pizzaiola or Marsala are dishes which require 24 hours notice.

Dom's offers a 5% discount for cash payment, which is certaily an incentive worth taking advantage of. Children dining with their parents before 6:30 p.m. may enjoy any entree for $4.00 less than the menu price, and senior citizens over 60 may order any meal for $2.00 less.

You only have to dine at Dom's to appreciate what Dom and Toni-Lee mean when they say that Italian food can be as elegant and refined as French food. The food at Dom's is light, delectable and well-presented and compares favorably with the best the Continent has to offer.

Dom's
337 Main Street
Hyannis, Mass. 02601
Telephone: 771-6213

Open: every day, yearround
Dinner: 5—11 p.m.
Seats: 43
Children's portions: at $4.00 less
than menu price before 6:30 p.m.

License: Beer & Wine
Credit cards: MC, VISA, AMEX
Parking: nearby parking lot
Reservations: Advised,
call 771-6213

Seafood Salad

Measure **1 cup of white wine** into a large pan with a lid.

Add **¾ lb. shrimp** and cook, covered, for about 5 minutes, or just until done. Strain, and save the broth.

In the same broth, cook **1 lb. scallops** for about 5 minutes, or just until done. Strain, and save the broth

In the same broth, cook **2 lbs. squid,** *whole,* plus the tentacles, for about 5 minutes, or just until done. Strain, and save the broth.

Poach open **12 littlenecks** (scrub them first) in the broth, then poach open **2 lbs.** mussels. Remove both the littlenecks and the mussels from their shells. Wash each mussel in the broth one at a time, being sure that the inside has been cleaned thoroughly.

Chop each shrimp into two or three pieces, and slice the scallops and squid into thin slices (cut the squid into rings).

Put all the seafood together. Add **½ teaspoon salt, ½ teaspoon pepper, 2 cloves garlic, crushed, ½ cup chopped parsley, ½ cup olive oil,** and a scant **¼ cup lemon juice.** Toss to mix. Taste for seasoning. Add more lemon juice or olive oil if needed to keep the seafood moist.

Garnish with **gremolata** and toss with extra olive oil and lemon juice just before serving.

Spaghetti Carbonara

Serves 4

6 **egg yolks**
¾ **cup heavy cream**
¼ **teaspoon pepper**
½ **teaspoon salt**
¼ **cup (4 oz.) pancetta, cubed (lean bacon may be substituted)**
¾ **cup (6 oz.) butter**
Fresh pasta, cooked *al dente,* **to serve 4**
Parmesan cheese to taste

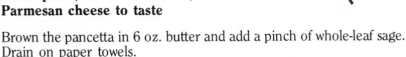

Brown the pancetta in 6 oz. butter and add a pinch of whole-leaf sage. Drain on paper towels.

Let the butter cool off, add it to the egg yolks and cream and stir well to mix.

For each order of pasta, measure into a frying pan a scant half cup of the mixture, and add a heaping soupspoon of freshly-grated Parmesan cheese. Add pasta, stir and heat through.

Serve hot, garnished with pancetta and extra cheese on the side. You may also use chopped walnuts as a garnish.

Scampi

Serves 4

12 **jumbo shrimp, deveined**
1 **stick (4 oz.) butter**
2 **cloves garlic, crushed**
1 **teaspoon tarragon**
2 **shallots, finely chopped**
1 **scallion, chopped**
Juice from ¼ lemon

Melt the butter slowly so it doesn't turn brown. Mix all ingredients, except the shrimp, with the butter and pour over the jumbo shrimp in a shallow, oven-proof pan.

Sprinkle the shrimp with kosher salt and broil under a high flame for about 3 minutes or until the shrimp turn pink. Turn over, baste with the sauce and repeat.

Impudent Oyster

Ask any Chatham resident which is his favorite eating spot and chances are he'll tell you it's the Impudent Oyster. Known for its innovative menu and informal atmosphere, the Impudent Oyster has been the favorite haunt of locals and visitors, both young and not-so-young, for seven years.

Peter and Michele Barnard, owners and managers, feel they were most fortunate to find two such excellent and experienced chefs as Bryan Jenkins and Heidi Schuetz, who between them handle a wide-ranging cuisine with dashing self-confidence . . . from fresh local seafood, Cape Cod specialties and New England favorites to more exotic fare that has strong Latin and Oriental overtones. The assortment of novelties offered includes Shrimp Mykonos, Chicken Porcini, Clams & Shrimp Romesco, Chinaman's Chance (baby shrimp, Chinese noodles and fresh vegetables in a mildly-spiced Hunan-style sauce), Shrimp Chiaretto (see following recipe), and Frogs Legs Marseille.

There are two distinctly different menus for summer and winter—the winter menu features plenty of pasta dishes, including Tortellini di Vitello, Sausage and Pasta Casserole or Pasta Volare made with hot or sweet locally-made sausage. And on damp Cape Cod winter days, spicy Mexican and Chinese specialties will chase the chills away. The summer menu offers a wide variety of fresh seafood from Chatham's fishing fleet, including Hunan Bluefish (see following recipe), Pesce fra Diablo and the Catch of the Day. Whatever the season, Wellfleet oysters appear on the menu in many guises—on the half-shell, fried, Oysters Casino, Celestial Oysters (see following recipe), in Szechwan Beef and Oyster saute, or simmered with other fresh seafood in the house specialty, a hearty Bouillabaisse. The chefs at the Impudent Oyster enjoy experimenting and creating new dishes so the seasonal menus and yearround daily lunch and dinner specials inevitably reflect their philosophy that food should never be boring.

Peter and Michele Barnard summered for many years in Chatham whilst working in restaurant management in Boston before opening The Impudent Oyster. They felt a restaurant offering a variety of authentic dishes from many different cultures in friendly surroundings would be a winning formula on the Cape . . . add reasonable prices to the list and you have an unbeatable combination.

The Impudent Oyster is located in down-town Chatham, right next to the Kate Gould Park where traditional Friday night Chatham Band concerts take place in the Park gazebo. The entrance to the dining room is through an old oak door set with antique leaded glass and an ornate 19th century bronze door handle. Inside, the restaurant has been decorated with turn-of-the-century stained glass panels and contemporary skylights in a beamed cathedral ceiling. The atmosphere is full of life and laughter—people come here for a good time as well as a good meal. As it true with all good restaurants on the Cape, the Impudent Oyster is busy in the summer months so reservations are a necessity for dinner.

The Impudent Oyster

15 Chatham Bars Avenue
Chatham, Mass. 02633
Telephone: 945-3545

Open: year round, seven days a week
      Summer: 11:30 to 3 and 5:30 to 10
      Winter: 11:30 to 3 and 6 to 9
Seats: 70
Bar: 11:30 to 1 a.m. weekdays;
      and noon to 1 a.m. Sundays
Credit cards: AMEX, MC, VISA
Parking: Adjacent lot and street parking
Reservations: Dinner reservations recommended, call 945-3545

Drunken Mussels

Serves 6 to 8

5 dozen mussels
1 cup water
1 cup tamari
1½ cup saki
1 cup sugar
1 oz. fresh grated ginger
1 tablespoon ground Szechwan peppers

Scrub mussels thoroughly and remove beards. Steam mussels in water until they open. Remove mussels from their liquor with a slotted spoon. Return stock to stove-top and reduce to 1 level cup liquid. Remove mussels from their shells and set aside.

Add remaining ingredients to reduced mussel liquor. Toss mussels in liquor and let stand in covered container overnight. Serve mussels with sauce on the side and garnish with grated daikon and wasabi (Japanese horseradish).

Mexican Chicken Chili and Lime Soup

Serves 6 to 8

6 cups rich chicken stock
10 green chilies, diced
3 large ripe tomatoes, peeled and diced
1 small onion, diced
2 large jalepeno peppers, diced
1 lb. canned tomatillos, diced
1 cup cooked, shredded chicken meat
8 artichoke hearts, chopped
Juice of 2 limes
1 tablespoon freshly ground cumin
1 tablespoon chopped fresh cilantro
2 tablespoons chopped fresh parsley

Place all ingredients in a soup pot and cook slowly until heated through. To serve: spoon soup into individual oven-proof soup bowls, top with fried corn tortilla chips and grated Muenster cheese and broil until cheese is bubbly. Serve immediately.

Celestial Oysters

Serves 6

2 lbs. freshly-shucked oysters
4 tablespoons butter
4 large shallots, diced
1 cup champagne
½ cup heavy cream
3 tablespoons roux
1½ cups Hollandaise sauce

Saute shallots quickly in hot butter over high heat. Add oysters and heat through. Add champagne and reduce quickly (do not overcook oysters). Remove oysters from pan with a slotted spoon and set aside.

Add cream and roux to pan juices and whisk thoroughly to make a smooth sauce. Return oysters to pan, heat through, remove pan from heat and quickly whisk in warmed Hollandaise sauce. Serve on a bed of pasta, preferably vermicelli. Garnish with freshly-ground black pepper.

Sicilian Veal Roast   Serves 6 to 8

6 or 7 lb. veal roast, rolled and tied
⅔ cups olive oil
1 tablespoon basil
1 tablespoon thyme
1 tablespoon oregano
1 teaspoon each rosemary, salt and pepper
2 tablespoons fresh lemon juice
1 tablespoon chopped fresh parsley
½ lb. thinly sliced prosciutto
1 lb. grated Bel Paese cheese
1 cup Marsala wine
2 cups veal demi-glaze
4 oz. cold butter

Untie and unroll veal roast. Trim off excess fat. Sprinkle the inside of the meat with ½ cup of the olive oil. Rub with most of the herbs, except the parsley, reserving a pinch of each herb for the top of the roast. Layer the ham and cheese on the veal. Roll up and retie the roast.

Place roast on a rack in a roasting pan. Sprinkle with remaining oil and herbs. Pour lemon juice and half of the wine over the meat. Bake at 350 degrees for 1½ hours or until the inside is pink. Baste frequently with pan juices and remaining wine. Remove roast and rack from roasting pan and keep warm. Place roasting pan on burners, add demi-glaze and reduce by ⅓. Swirl in cold butter and parsley. Heat through and stir. Pour sauce over sliced pieces of roast and serve.

Hunan Bluefish

Serves 6 to 8

2 or 3 lbs. fresh bluefish fillets
⅔ cups Kikkoman soy sauce
⅓ cup dry sherry
½ cup sugar
4 large cloves garlic, diced
1 oz. fresh grated ginger
1½ cups freshly squeezed orange juice

2 or 3 diced Hunan chilies
¼ cup garlic butter
1 bunch scallions, slivered

Combine soy sauce, sherry, sugar, garlic and ginger in a small saucepan. Bring to a boil and remove from heat immediately. Add orange juice and chilies and cool.

Place fish fillets on a baking dish, dot with garlic butter, pour sauce over fillets and arrange scallions on top. Bake for 20 or 25 minutes in the oven at 425 degrees.

Enchilada Verde

Serves 6 to 8

1 large green pepper, roasted and peeled
1 small tomato, peeled
2 small cloves garlic
1 small onion, roughly chopped
1½ lb. tomatillos, canned
2 jalepenos, chopped
1 tablespoon fresh cilantro, chopped
Pinch of cumin
1¼ lb. low moisture mozzarella cheese
1 cup finely diced onion
18 corn tortillas
½ lb. farmer cheese
Sour cream

Put first 8 ingredients in a blender and blend to make a smooth sauce. Cut mozzarella into 18 equal strips. Steam tortillas until pliable. Place 1 strip of cheese in center of tortilla and sprinkle with diced onion. Roll tortilla tightly and place seam side down in a shallow baking dish. Follow same procedure with remaining tortillas, cheese and onion. Pour sauce over all, sprinkle with farmer cheese and bake in oven at 350 degrees for 20 or 25 minutes or until cheese has melted. Garnish with sour cream.

La Grande Rue

The Old Kemah Inn is a rambling old building on Main Street, Harwich-port, which dates from the 1870s. It has been operating as an inn since the early 1900s, but La Grande Rue, the restaurant named after the road it overlooks, has only been in existence since 1977. The owner and manager of both the inn and restaurant is Stephen Vining, a refugee from city living and the corporate rat race who had always loved the Cape and seized the opportunity to move here when the occasion arose.

The restaurant started in a very small way in the room that is now the bar; it has grown in size over the years, gradually taking over more and more of the downstairs rooms of the inn, so it now can seat 90 people. Recently, Stephen extended the dining area into the glassed-in porch which overlooks the sidewalk, adding to the illusion that this is an old French country roadside inn.

Inside, the dining rooms are charmingly quaint and old-fashioned in the old-fashioned sense . . . walls unadorned save for print wallpaper, tables laid with cream-colored linens, candles and fresh flowers, and a different set of old dark wood dining chairs at each table. A comfortable atmosphere for enjoying a satisfying meal, and one fairly unique on Cape Cod where "old-fashioned Cape Cod" so often leans towards the contrived.

Stephen Vining, the chef, has always loved cooking and is self-taught, his repertoire and skill having increased as the size of his restaurant has grown. The richly-varied menu of classical French dishes contains 20 main courses from which to choose, each dish prepared to order. In the seafood category there is Lobster, prepared any way you wish, Scallop and Mussel Royale (see following recipe), Moules Mariniere,

Bouillabaisse and Oysters de Jonge; steaks include Entrecote au Poivre, Boeuf aux Artichauts, Chateaubriand, and Tournedos a la Grande Rue (see following recipe); other specialties on the menu are Veal au Calvados, Frogs Legs Provencale, and Duck in a Black Cherry Sauce. Stephen's father-in-law, who is of French extraction, helps with baking fresh bread and makes the many desserts . . . Crepes du Jour, Chocolate Mousse, Homemade Fresh Fruit Sorbets, Homemade Cheesecake, Gateau Chocolat.

Since opening his restaurant, Stephen has enthusiastically adopted wine sampling as a hobby, so the wine list, with over 60 varieties, is likely to cater to the most discriminating taste. The selection is heavy on white Burgundy, red Bordeaux, California Chardonnay and Cabernet Sauvignon—wines which Stephen has found to be the most frequently requested. The house wine is a French Bordeaux. There is also an extensive list of brandies and Cognacs to choose from, as well as liqueur coffee mixed any way you could possibly wish for.

At La Grande Rue you'll find low-key candlelit dining amid pleasant surroundings—and a chef who strives for consistency. His aim is to present each dish individually prepared with as much care as you would find anywhere, and to be able to maintain the same high standard each and every time.

La Grande Rue
at The Old Kemah Inn
551 Main Street (Route 28)
Harwichport, MA
Telephone: 432-1306

Open: Every day in season; closed Mon. & Tues. off season.
Lunch: 12 to 3
Dinner: 6 to 10
Seats: 90
Children's portions: not available
License: Full liquor license
Credit cards: AMEX, MC, VISA
Parking: large parking lot nearby
Reservations: Advised, call 432-1306

Oysters Parmesan   Serves 6

---

3 dozen freshly-shucked oysters
2 cups dry white wine
3 tablespoons finely chopped shallots

---

1 tablespoon fresh tarragon
1 tablespoon mustard seeds
1 quart heavy cream
4 egg yolks
3 tablespoons Bechamel sauce
Salt and pepper to taste

Place wine, shallots, tarragon and seasonings in a saucepan and simmer until reduced by half. Whisk in 3 tablespoons Bechamel sauce until smooth. Whip in 1 quart of heavy cream and 4 egg yolks and heat gently until thickened.

Place mixture in shucked oysters on the half shell. Bake on rock salt in the oven at 350 degrees for 8 or 10 minutes.

Soupe au Moules (Mussel Soup)　　　Serves 8

2 quarts mussels
½ cup dry white wine
2 tablespoons chopped parsley
3 oz. butter
2 medium onions, finely chopped
2 cloves garlic, crushed
½ cup hot milk
2 egg yolks
½ cup cream
3 cups boiling water
Juice of 1 lemon
8 small pieces toasted French bread
Salt and pepper
Bouquet garni

Scrub mussels thoroughly and remove beards. Steam mussels open in ½ cup white wine and one clove of garlic. Strain broth. Saute onions and one clove of garlic in butter in a saucepan. When onions are translucent, add strained mussel broth, bouquet garni, chopped parsley, 3 cups boiling water and ½ cup hot milk. Simmer gently for 15 minutes. Add shelled mussels and simmer for a few more minutes. Season to taste.

Beat egg yolks, cream and the juice of one lemon in a large bowl or soup tureen. Pour mussel soup over the egg and cream mixture, stirring as you add the soup. Serve with toasted French bread as a garnish.

Scallops & Mussels Royal

Per person:

5 oz. scallops
1 oz. sliced fresh mushrooms
10 mussels, scrubbed, debearded, steamed and shelled
Juice of ½ lemon
Pinch of fresh parsley, chopped
½ oz. malt whisky

1 oz. heavy cream
1 clove shallots, minced
1 oz. unsalted butter

Place butter, mushrooms, scallops and shallots in a saute pan and slowly cook for 2 or 3 minutes. Add the whisky and flame. When flame has subsided, add the cream, parsley, lemon juice and mussels. Cook slowly until cream thickens.

Poulet Romanichel

Per person:

8 oz. boneless chicken breast, skin removed
2 thin slices Gruyere cheese
2 thin slices baked ham
2 oz. olive oil
1 tablespoon minced garlic
1 teaspoon shallots, minced
1 tablespoon parsley
¼ cup dry white wine
1 cup milk, 1 cup flour and 1 cup cornmeal, sifted for breading chicken breasts

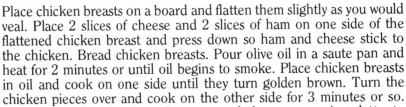

Place chicken breasts on a board and flatten them slightly as you would veal. Place 2 slices of cheese and 2 slices of ham on one side of the flattened chicken breast and press down so ham and cheese stick to the chicken. Bread chicken breasts. Pour olive oil in a saute pan and heat for 2 minutes or until oil begins to smoke. Place chicken breasts in oil and cook on one side until they turn golden brown. Turn the chicken pieces over and cook on the other side for 3 minutes or so.

Remove chicken pieces from pan and place on a serving platter to keep warm. Pour off half the oil remaining in pan and deglaze pan with the wine. Add the parsley, garlic and shallots. Reduce by ⅓ and pour sauce over chicken breasts and serve.

Tournedos a La Grande Rue

Per person:
9 oz. (approximately) piece of beef tenderloin, trimmed
2 slices bacon
½ teaspoon garlic, minced
½ teaspoon shallots, minced
½ teasoon chopped parsley
1 oz. unsalted butter

Flatten tenderloin pieces slightly and cut each piece into three vertical slices, approximately ¼" thick. Put the three pieces back together again (the meat cooks more evenly when cut this way) and wrap two pieces of bacon around the meat. Secure with toothpicks. Broil tenderloin to personal preference.

Melt butter in a saute pan and add shallots, garlic and parsley. Cook over a low heat until garlic and shallots are cooked. Be careful not to burn. Pour sauce over broiled tenderloin and serve.

Frozen Chocolate Crepes   Makes 12

Chocolate Mousse mixture:
4 eggs
½ lb. dark semi-sweet chocolate
2 tablespoons melted butter
1 teaspoon vanilla essence
1 teaspoon (more if you wish)
Grand Marnier liqueur

Crepe mixture:
1 cup milk
½ cup flour
¼ cup sugar

Beat together milk, sifted flour and sugar, cover and refrigerate for a few minutes. Make crepes in a seasoned crepe pan and let them cool between sheets of waxed paper.

Separate the eggs and lightly beat the egg yolks. Melt the chocolate in a double boiler and gently stir in the egg yolks. Add vanilla essence and liqueur and let the mixture cool slightly.

Beat the egg whites until they form stiff peaks. Fold the egg whites into the chocolate mixture, but do not over mix.

Fill each crepe with a spoonful of chocolate mixture, roll up and place on a cookie sheet. Cover with film wrap and freeze.

Serve frozen garnished with shaved chocolate and a splash of Cream de Cocoa.

The Old Manse Inn

The Old Manse Inn, sitting snugly among a group of tall chestnut trees on Main Street, Brewster, epitomizes the enduring charm of old Cape Cod. This former sea captain's home, built in the early 1800s by Captain William Lewis Knowles, has been operating as an inn since 1945, and was purchased by its present owners, Douglas and Sugar Manchester, in 1979. They renovated the inn's 10 guest rooms, decorating them with antiques, handmade quilts and period furniture.

The Manchesters' son, Cliff, runs the dining room with Ruth Besse, a project they enthusiastically embarked upon in December 1981 and which has, in the short time since, attracted a sizeable following and an excellent reputation. Cliff and Ruth are both basically self-taught, and have had many years experience in the kitchens of several first-rate restaurants in the neighborhood. They are assisted in the kitchen by Greg, Cliff's younger brother, while Elise, Ruth's daughter, attends to bus duties.

The dining room was at one time a chapel for the Lutheran Church, and was later converted into a solarium. Its unusual shape and beautiful proportions are perfectly suited to its present use. It seats only 20 or so, but a limited overflow can be accommodated in the adjoining drawing room. Dinner is by reservation only and the table is booked for the entire evening; seating is between 7 and 8 p.m. The table settings are especially attractive, with arrangements of fresh flowers gathered from The Old Manse's gardens, and lighted by tall candles beneath glass globes. An added pleasure to dining at The Old Manse Inn is being able to eat off fine antique porcelain—there's a different design for each table. Dessert is served on hand-painted German china plates, and coffee is poured into gilded Royal Worcester cups, all perfectly in keeping with the mood and character of the surroundings.

The menu at The Old Manse is unusually creative and changes frequently. Ruth and Cliff pride themselves in using the freshest ingredients obtainable, personally selecting their meat, fish and produce each morning for that night's menu. As everything is prepared and baked the same day it is served, the menu is limited--there are three appetizers or soups to choose from, three entrees and three desserts. In the summer the menu changes weekly, and guests may choose either a prix-fixe dinner for $23 (choice of appetizer or soup; entree with fresh homemade rolls, salad and fresh vegetables; dessert and coffee), or a six course dinner for $28, which also includes a homemade sherbet and a Grande Dessert —a taste of all three of the evening's dessert offerings. An eight-course meal may also be ordered in advance for $35.

Certain dishes have become especially popular with regular visitors and these crop up more frequently on the menu–they include Tenderloin of Beef with a Roquefort and White Wine Sauce, Salmon Rose with Saffron-Basil Beurre Blanc Sauce (see following recipe) and an Orange Almond Tarte, the recipe for which has been requested by Gourmet Magazine (recipe follows). The gardens of The Old Manse provide fresh herbs for sauces and flavorings in the summer, and window sill pots serve the same purpose in winter.

Just recently, The Old Manse received a beer and wine license so Doug and Sugar Manchester are laying in a fine selection of imported wine, chosen carefully to complement the varied flavors of the dishes served in the dining room.

The Old Manse Inn is a delightful place to visit, both in the dead of winter when comfortable sofas and crackling fires tempt you in from the cold, and in the summer when cool breezes whisper in the tall trees. The fine food and sympathetic surroundings ensure that visitors to The Old Manse will not be disappointed . . . in fact, customers have often told Ruth Besse that eating in her restaurant is like being a guest at an elegant dinner party.

Old Manse Inn — "Dinner at The Manse"
1861 Main Street
Brewster, MA 02631
Telephone: 896-3149

Open year round: Tuesday through Saturday, in season
    Thursday, Friday & Saturday during September
    Friday & Saturday during October & November
Closed: Sunday & Monday, and during December except for special parties
Dinner: by reservation *only*—one seating between 7 and 8
Seats: 30
Children's portions: not available
License: Beer & Wine
Credit cards: AMEX, MC, VISA
Parking: ample private parking
Reservations: necessary, call 896-3149

Scallop Bisque with Caviar

Serves 4

1 lb. scallops, rinsed and trimmed
(make sure tough mussel filament on side is removed)
1 shallot, finely minced
3 tablespoons (1½ oz.) unsalted butter
3 tablespoons flour
2 cups chicken stock
2 cups fish stock
½ cup dry white wine
2 egg yolks
½ cup heavy cream
Pinch cayenne
American Golden Caviar or lumpfish caviar to garnish

Saute shallots in butter until they are translucent. Add flour and stir over low heat for 8 minutes—do not let roux brown. Combine chicken and fish stocks in a saucepan and bring to a boil, removing scum if necessary. Add stock to roux gradually, whisking the mixture over a low flame. Season with cayenne and strain.

Puree scallops in a food processor and add to the soup. Whisk heavy cream and egg yolks together and pour 2 ladles of the soup onto the egg and cream mixture, whisking well as it is added. Return this mixture to the soup and heat through. Thin with light cream if necessary. Garnish with caviar just before serving.

This soup is also delightful chilled and garnished with chopped fresh coriander and a slice of lime.

Fettucine with Mushrooms and Hearts of Artichoke

Serves 4

Pasta:

4 cups flour
4 eggs
Dash of salt

Mix ingredients together to form an elastic dough. Cover with a damp cloth and let the dough rest for 30 minutes. Cut it into four pieces and put through the thinnest rollers of a pasta machine. Cut into noodles. Just before serving, cook for one or so minutes in boiling salted water until *al dente*.

Sauce:

3 large fresh tomatoes, peeled,
    seeded and chopped finely
½ cup dry white wine
1 tablespoon minced shallots
1 clove garlic, minced
1 teaspoon each of fresh thyme, oregano
    and parsley, chopped
1 cup sliced mushrooms
4 large artichoke hearts, cooked and quartered
4 oz. unsalted butter
Salt and pepper to taste

Saute mushrooms, shallots, garlic and herbs in 2 tablespoons butter until mushrooms are cooked. Raise heat and add wine. Reduce to half volume. Add tomatoes and reduce to a thick sauce. Lower heat and add remaining butter, ½ oz. at a time, and season to taste. Add artichoke hearts and heat through.

    Ladle sauce over pasta and sprinkle with freshly-grated Parmesan cheese. (You may freeze any extra pasta for use at a later date.)

Grilled Breast of Duckling with Beach Plums

Serves 4

---

2 4—5 lb. ducklings
4 cups good duck stock
½ cup fresh beach plums
4 tablespoons (2 oz.) unsalted butter
Beach plum jelly
Clarified butter

Remove breast meat from ducklings. Remove layer of fat and skin from breast meat and set aside. Remove leg/thigh sections and roast them for 20 minutes at 500 degrees on a rack. Set aside and keep warm.

    Reduce duck stock until it coats a spoon and is slightly sticky. Add the beach plums and cook until they are soft and exuding juices. Strain. Swirl in the butter, 1 tablespoon at a time. Taste for seasoning and add the beach plum jelly to taste, 1 teaspoon at a time.

    Brush the duck breast with clarified butter and quickly grill the meat over hot coals until just medium rare (do not overcook). Place leg/thigh sections on a grill to heat through and crisp skin slightly. Slice breast meat and serve with a roasted leg over sauce.

Salmon Rose with Saffron/Basil Beurre Blanc

Serves 4

4 salmon steaks, 1" thick
1 cup dry white wine
6 tablespoons (3 oz.) unsalted butter
¼ cup heavy cream
1 shallot, finely minced
1 tablespoon white wine vinegar
1 saffron thread
Fresh basil leaves
Parchment paper

To prepare fish: remove center bones with a sharp knife and cut steaks in half down the center. Skin the steaks and pull out any small bones with tweezers. Slice the salmon into strips ¼" thick by 1" wide. Fold a 10" piece of parchment paper in half and butter the inside. Shape salmon strips into a rose shape on the paper and seal. Bake for 6 or 8 minutes on a cookie sheet at 500 degrees.

To make the sauce: combine the wine, heavy cream, vinegar and shallots and cook until reduced by half. Add butter, 1 tablespoon at a time, whisking constantly. Grind saffron thread in a mortar and add to sauce. Stack about a dozen large basil leaves together and roll them up jelly-roll style. Slice roll of basil leaves thinly to form chiffonade of basil. Add to sauce and heat through. Ladle sauce onto heated plates. Remove salmon roses from their parchment envelopes and carefully place over the sauce. Garnish with a fresh basil leaf.

Strawberries in Cranberry Honey with Cranberry Liqueur

Serves 4

1 pint fresh strawberries
3 tablespoons cranberry honey
¼ cup Boggs cranberry liqueur
Whipped cream and shaved bittersweet chocolate

Hull strawberries and slice larger berries in half. Macerate in a glass or cermic bowl with the honey and liqueur. Chill. Serve in individual bowls garnished with sweetened whipped cream and shaved chocolate.

Orange Almond Tarte

Pastry:

1 cup flour
1 egg yolk
3 oz. unsalted butter
3 tablespoons sugar
1 tablespoon ice water
Dash of cinnamon
Dash of salt

Combine all ingredients in a food processor until they form a lump of dough. Roll out dough on a floured board and shape pastry into a flan pan with a removable ring. Chill for 10 minutes in the freezer.

Line the flan case with foil and baking beads or rice and bake for 10 minutes at 375 degrees. Remove foil and beads and bake for 5 minutes more. Cool.

Filling:

1½ cups almonds
½ cup sugar (generous)
2 tablespoons flour
4 large navel oranges
Grand Marnier liqueur
Orange marmalade
Whipped cream to garnish

Process almonds, sugar and flour until fine. Peel and section oranges over a bowl, collecting juice in the bowl. Drain orange sections on paper towels. Add 2 tablespoons Grand Marnier to reserved juice and add to almond-sugar mixture. Mix well and spread onto crust. Bake at 400 degrees for 10 or 15 minutes.

Cool tarte. Arrange orange sections on top of filling. Heat marmalade and paint over oranges. Serve garnished with sweetened whipped cream.

Penguins Go Pasta
at Three-Thirty One

Look for the sign of the penguin on Main Street, Hyannis, and you'll discover behind the brick facade and canopied awnings a highly successful and efficiently run Italian restaraunt. Now owned by chef/manager Robert Gold and Elaine Karath, the restaurant has been owned by Robert Gold's family for 40 years; originally it was known at the College Grille and Oyster Bar, and later as the Fish Shanty. Robert Gold renamed and remodeled the restaurant and, on the strength of a lifetime's involvement in the family restaurant business and a degree from the Culinary Institute of America, opened the doors for business on May 19, 1981.

Penguins Go Pasta caters to people who appreciate good food and wine, and aims to serve classical Italian dishes prepared in the correct manner. Robert Gold, who is also an instructor in culinary arts at Cape Cod Community College and was a team member in 1982 of the Boston Epicurian Salon where his team won the Grand Buffet and Bronze National Medal, believes that quality foods, quality service and good organization comprise the formula for a successful restaurant. Working with these components and with a young and enthusiastic staff, the kitchen at Three Thirty One produces a consistently high standard of food both for the restaurant, which seats 125, and for a burgeoning catering business.

All the food served in the restaurant is made daily on the premises, including the pasta, the crusty breads and all desserts. One of the specialties of the house is freshly-made three-colored pasta—plain, tomato and spinach—which is available with a choice of sauce, including carbonara, vongole, aglio olio, al pesto. Other specialties include Braised Rabbit with Polenta, Veal Fontina, Osso Bucco (see following recipe), Lasagne "Penguino" and Frutti de Mare served over homemade linguine. All entrees come with a salad, fresh bread and a side order of the pasta of the day. The wine list contains a large selection from the major Italian regions as well as French and domestic varieties, and the house wines— Italian Principato, Californian (Mirassou) and a French red and white Bordeaux—are available by the carafe or the glass.

The interior at Three Thirty One has been beautifully designed to create an attractive dining room that is bright, cheerful and contemporary with just a touch of sophistication. Bare brick walls interspersed with mirrors and diagonal oak paneling form a backdrop for colorful framed prints and posters and lush hanging plants. A large raised dias in one corner of the dining room surrounded by brass railings and potted palms creates a separate dining section that is a little more formal than the rest. Tables are attractively laid with sparkling glassware and burgundy-colored linen, and waiters are cheerful, efficient and formally dressed— could this explain the penguin connection?

It's quite a coincidence that two of Cape Cod's finest Italian restaurants—and the only two that make their own pasta as far as I am aware—are situated side by side in downtown Hyannis. Both strive for equally high standards, yet both retain their own very personal style— and both are most certainly worth a visit.

Penguins Go Pasta
at Three Thirty-One
331 Main Street
Hyannis, Mass. 02601
Telephone: 775-2023

Open: every day, year round
Dinner: In season: 4 to 11 p.m.
        Off-season: 4 to 9 p.m. Sunday
        through Thursday and
        4 to 10 p.m. Friday & Saturday
Seats: 125
Children's portions: not available
License: full liquor license
Credit cards: AMEX, MC, VISA
Parking: public parking nearby
Reservations: for parties of 8 or more *only*.

Creamy Dill Salad Dressing

Makes 1 gallon

5 large eggs
3 quarts salad oil
1 pint lemon juice
½ pint wine vinegar
2 bunches fresh dill
2 oz. chopped fresh garlic
1 bunch fresh parsley, chopped
3 oz. jar Poupon Dijon mustard
2 tablespoons crushed black pepper

Place eggs in a mixing bowl. Add mustard and garlic and mix ingredients with an electric beater until they are well blended. Slowly add oil to the egg mix, drop by drop to start with, and then in a thin stream as it emulsifies. The dressing should be thick and creamy like mayonnaise.

Add the chopped dill and parsley, lemon juice, vinegar and pepper and mix in. Store in refrigerator and mix well before using.

Roasted Peppers & Eggplant

Serves 4

6 large green peppers
4 large red peppers
2 cloves garlic, crushed finely
1 small eggplant, diced
4 plum tomatoes, peeled, seeded and chopped
½ cup olive oil
Juice of 1 lemon

Char the peppers over an open flame until the skins blister all over. Peel peppers and discard the seeds. Slice the peppers into 1" slices and place in a bowl.

Pour olive oil into a saute pan. Saute eggplant until golden. Add garlic and tomatoes. Add lemon juice and all other ingredients. Mix together and add salt and pepper to taste. Serve chilled, garnished with lemon wedges.

Award-winning Mussels Dijon

Serves 4

5 lbs. mussels, scrubbed and de-bearded
1 pint heavy cream
½ pint white wine
1 carrot, grated
1 clove garlic, chopped finely
2 scallions, diced
½ stalk leek, diced
4 heaping tablespoons Poupon Dijon mustard
2 oz. olive oil

Place grated carrot, leek, garlic, and scallions in a 4 quart pot and saute lightly in olive oil. Add the mustard, mussels (in their shells), cream and wine and stir to mix. Cover pot and shake to make sure mussels are coated. Steam on high heat until mussels open. Cook for two minutes longer. Spoon into individual soup plates and serve with hot crusty bread. Enjoy!

Osso Bucco

Serves 4

8 pieces veal shank, cut into 1½" pieces
2 carrots, cut brunoise
2 celery stalks, cut brunoise
1 large onion, cut brunoise
½ teaspoon orange rind, finely diced
¼ teaspoon lemon peel, finely diced
1 teaspoon chopped garlic
1 pinch marjoram
6 plum tomatoes, peeled, seeded and chopped
1 cup white wine
1 cup glace de viande
4 oz. clarified butter
1 cup cooking oil
Salt and pepper to taste

Flour veal shanks and saute on both sides in oil. Place veal shanks in a casserole dish large enough to hold them without crowding.

Preheat the oven to 400 degrees. Pour off the fat in the saute pan and add the clarified butter. Saute the garlic, carrots, onion and celery in the butter until slightly transparent. Add the wine and reduce by three-quarters.

Add the orange and lemon rind and tomatoes and cook together for two minutes. Add the glace de viande to the pan. Heat the mixture and pour over the veal shanks.

Cover casserole dish and place in the oven. Cook for 1½ hours at 400 degrees. Taste and add seasoning and marjoram to taste. Osso Bucco may be served with any pasta, polenta or gnocchi dish.

Bananas Amaretto
Serves 4

4 bananas cut into 1" slices
1 cup brown sugar
1 stick unsalted butter
½ lemon
3 oz. dark rum
3 oz. Amaretto
Ice cream

Place butter and sugar in a saute pan and melt together until bubbly. Add bananas and saute for approximately 3 or 4 minutes.

Squeeze lemon juice from ½ lemon over the bananas. Add the rum and flame off the alcohol. Add the Amaretto and stir. Simmer for 2 or 3 minutes until flavors are well blended. Serve hot over ice cream.

The Regatta

The Regatta in Falmouth has probably the most spectacular waterfront location of any restaurant on the Cape. Situated at the end of Scranton Avenue, The Regatta is a low, grey-shingled building with a private 90' dock right at the entrance to Falmouth's beautiful inner harbor. Owners/managers Brantz and Wendy Bryan have created here an establishment that successfully combines first rate cuisine, exceptional service and a stunning decor.

Brantz and Wendy always enjoyed dining out from a very early age, and still do. The idea of living, working and playing right next to the water on Cape Cod appealed to them both and these factors, coupled with their love of fine food and their desire to be able to develop their own ideas, persuaded them that purchasing The Regatta would be a rewarding experience . . . and one that would provide a meaningful livlihood as the direct result of putting their ideas and labors into action. So they purchased The Regatta in 1969, which they still run as a seasonal business in order to keep up the level of energy and enthusiasm necessary to maintain the high standards they strive for.

At The Regatta, great emphasis is placed on quality of food ingredients, food preparation and service. The basic philosophy that binds kitchen, dining room and management personnel is that The Regatta is first and foremost dedicated to please the individual diner in every respect. Brantz and Wendy believe in offering their guests a wide and interesting choice of dishes; they aim to have a staff knowledgeable about the food served, and who are also able to recommend a wine from their stock of over 50 varieties that would most complement the chosen dish. To be certain this approach works, each waiter or waitress works directly with one of the chefs for a certain period of time so that they may learn, first hand, the many details of food production and preparation.

Brantz Bryan explains that "Good fresh food, carefully and well prepared and attractively presented, is the first priority of our restaurant . . . all our seafood, meats, produce and ingredients are purchased fresh and on the Cape whenever possible." The Regatta's kitchen staff, a young crew, mostly in their twenties, have for the most part chosen the restaurant business as their profession. Food preparation starts in the kichen at 7:30 a.m. and finishes as late as 11:00 p.m. due to the wide range of dishes on the menu—at least 11 different appetizers, 4 soups, 13 fish entrees, 7 meat dishes and 11 desserts, ranging from the simple but delicious to the more creative. Each entree is presented with a sampling of three different fresh vegetables, selected for their taste, shape and color and compatability with the main dish. Garnishes are colorful and added with an artistic flourish.

The menu is mostly made up of "specialties"—that is, items that have been offered as special dishes in the past and which, due to their popularity, have been added to the regular menu. This menu is regularly overhauled—new specialties replace less popular items if they were met with an enthusiastic response. Just a few of these dishes are Filet of Sole Princess Diana (with crabmeat and Parmesan cheese, topped with Champagne sauce), Scallops Osterville (scallops marinated in British ale and sauteed with walnuts in butter, tarragon vinegar and cream), Tournedos Troisgros, and Sweetbreads & Lobster Meat Sippewisset (boneless breast of chicken filled with Boursin cheese and a mushroom duxelle, baked in parchment paper and served with a white wine sauce).

A word must be said about The Regatta's luscious table settings—raspberry tablecloths, crisp pink napkins displayed in sparkling wine glasses, and lovely hand-blown glass lamps. This color scheme is repeated throughout the interior and exterior of the restaurant in the many hanging baskets of pink and white geraniums and pots of hot pink impatiens.

The Bryans are justifiably proud of the fact that their establishment has grown and prospered over the years on the strength of good food and fine wine—they serve no beer or liquor—and also because for the past six years or so they have been awarded three-star status by several respected Boston dining critics.

The Regatta
End of Scranton Avenue
Falmouth, Mass. 02540
Telephone: 548-5400

Rated ★ ★ ★

Open: late May until late September,
    seven nights a week
Dinner: 5:30 to 10:00
Seats: 120
Children's portions: not available
License: Wine only
Credit cards: AMEX, MC, VISA
Parking: private parking in front and adjacent parking lot
Reservations: Advised, call 548-5400

Chilled Watercress & Leek Soup   Serves 6—8

This soup is best made the day before you plan to serve it.

2 large baking potatoes, peeled and diced
2 cups rich chicken stock
1½ cups diced leeks, white part only
4 oz. butter
2 cups light cream
4 bundles watercress, stems removed
Chopped chives
Salt, white pepper and nutmeg

Saute leeks in butter in a 6 quart pot until they are transparent (about 5 or 6 minutes). Add potatoes and stock. Cook until potatoes are over-done and mushy. Season to taste. Place mixture in a food processor and puree, then push through a small hole strainer. This is a lot easier when the mixture is hot. Refrigerate overnight.

Place the light cream and watercress in a food processor and puree until all the leaves are finely ground. Add this to the potato base. You may need more cream depending on how thick you wish the soup to be.

Garnish soup with chopped chives and a pinch of nutmeg. Serve with a wedge of lime.

Saffron Vermicelli with
Smoked Mussels & Peas   Serves 6—8

1 lb. saffron pasta
1 pt. smoked mussels
1 cup frozen green peas
4 oz. butter
¼ cup Gorgonzola cheese, grated
¼ cup Parmesan cheese, grated
¼ cup Italian Fontina cheese, grated
Salt and freshly-ground black pepper
Nutmeg
3 cups heavy cream
1 egg yolk

Cook pasta in plenty of boiling, salted water. Strain and cool. Melt butter in a large saute pan and add smoked mussels. Toss and add pasta. Sprinkle with black pepper. Add peas and heavy cream and stir a little until cream has warmed through. Add cheese and nutmeg. Be careful as this will scorch very easily

If sauce becomes too thick add more cream and adjust seasonings. Stir in egg yolk and remove pot from heat. Serve on 6" plates, topped with grated Parmesan cheese and chopped parsley.

Shrimp & Scallop Serviche   Serves 4

8 oz. raw shrimp, deveined and shelled
8 oz. scallops (cut sea scallops in half)
1 small red onion, chopped
1 large green pepper, chopped
1 cup olive oil
¼ cup wine vinegar
¼ cup white wine
¼ cup fresh lemon juice
Salt, white pepper, bay leaf, thyme,
    chervil and basil

Place shrimp, scallops and chopped vegetables in a stainless steel bowl. Put remaining ingredients for marinade in a heavy pot and bring to a boil. Pour boiling marinade over seafood, toss and let stand at room temperature until cooled. Refrigerate for 24 hours. Stir occasionally to make sure all seafood is marinating.

Remove seafood with a slotted spoon and serve on a bed of Boston lettuce. Garnish with a cherry tomato, lemon or lime wedges and fresh dill.

Medallions of Striped Bass
with Cider & Cream   Serves 4

6 oz. striped bass per person
    (3 or 4 medallions)
12 apple slices
6 shallots, minced
1 cup dry cider
1 cup heavy fish stock, warmed
1½ cups heavy cream
Salt, white pepper, bay leaf,
    pinch of thyme and nutmeg
1 teaspoon diced fresh ginger
3 oz. butter

The success of this dish depends on not overcooking the fish and being careful not to reduce the cider to the point where it might become bitter.

Filet the bass and remove the skin. Cut medallions by starting to cut the fish at the large end. Hold the knife at a slight angle and cut ¼" slices. When you get towards the tail you may find it necessary to butterfly each piece.

Dredge fish in flour, melt the butter and saute medallions lightly for a few minutes. Remove fish. Add apple slices and cook for long enough to warm them through. Place 3 slices of apple on each plate with three of four pieces of bass and keep warm.

Add shallots and ginger to pan and saute lightly, adding more butter if necessary. Do not brown. Deglaze the pan with the cider and add seasonings. Add hot fish stock and cream and reduce slowly by half, being careful not to scorch the sauce. Adjust seasoning and whip in 1 teaspoon of unsalted butter. Strain sauce over fish and garnish with fresh dill.

Rack of Lamb with Anise and Sweet Garlic

Serves 4

Do not be alarmed at the amount of garlic used in this recipe—I have found that cooking the garlic in the skin results in a very sweet taste, rather than the stronger and more bitter flavor which results from crushing the garlic. When buying the racks of lamb, make sure that the chine bone is sawed off by the butcher so the chops may be carved easily.

2 racks of lamb, split and chined
Coarse salt and freshly-ground black pepper
2¼ teaspoons anise seed
2 heads of garlic, separated but unpeeled
½ cup port wine
4 cups lamb or beef stock

Preheat oven to 425 degrees. Season each rack of lamb with one teaspoon of anise and salt and pepper and rub meat with one clove of peeled garlic. Place lamb in a roasting pan without a rack. Spread the garlic cloves around the lamb and roast for 45 to 55 minutes, depending on personal taste. Remove lamb and keep in a warm place.

Place roasting pan on top of burner. Remove the skin from the garlic cloves and mash them with a wooden spoon in the pan. Skim as much fat off from the pan as you can and add the last ¼ teaspoon anise seed to the pan along with the port and stock. Bring this to a boil and reduce until it turns to a syrupy consistency, skimming off any excess fat. Strain sauce.

To serve, simply carve the lamb in single chops, ladle sauce on warmed plates and place lamb chops on top of sauce. Garnish with fresh mint leaves.

Breast of Chicken with Chestnut Puree & Chanterelles   Serves 4

These chicken breasts may be stuffed a day before serving.

4 8-oz. chicken breasts, boned and skinned
1 cup chestnut puree (from canned or fresh nuts)
2 shallots, finely diced
1 small can chanterelles, washed and drained
    or quartered fresh mushrooms
1 cup chicken stock
1½ cups glace de viande
¾ cup Madeira (Sherry may be substituted)
Heavy cream
Salt and freshly-ground black pepper
Sage and nutmeg
Seasoned flour

Puree chestnuts in a blender or food processor if you are using canned nuts; if you are using fresh chestnuts, boil them in water with a little sugar added to it. Save some of the liquid to add to the puree if it's too dry. Peel the chestnuts. Place them in a food processor and puree them. Add sage and nutmeg to the chestnut puree to taste.

Trim excess fat from chicken breasts. Place them between sheets of plastic wrap and flatten with a mallet or the side of a cleaver just enough to ensure even cooking. (It is important to keep the chicken breasts in one piece.) Spread a small handful of chestnut puree over one side of the chicken breast. Fold the other side over and press down with your hand to seal in the puree. Heat a 10" or 12" saute pan and cover the bottom with oil. Dredge chicken pieces in seasoned flour and sautee in oil for about two or three minutes on each side, making sure they don't brown too much. Remove chicken breasts from pan and keep warm.

Add shallots and chanterelles or mushrooms to pan and saute lightly in a little butter. Deglaze the pan with Madeira wine, reduce enough to burn off the alcohol and add the chicken stock and the glace de viande. Remove any particles of food in the bottom of the pan with a whisk. Reduce the sauce until it takes on a light, syrupy consistency. Add a touch of heavy cream and sweet butter and ladle the sauce and chanterelles over the chicken pieces. Garnish with watercress.

Frozen Cassis Mousse   Serves 6—8

40 homemade or imported lady fingers
½ cup cassis (blackcurrant liqueur)
⅔ cup sugar
⅓ cup blackcurrants
⅓ cup blackcurrant syrup
4 egg yolks
1¾ cups heavy cream

Soak the lady fingers in half of the cassis. Combine the blackcurrant syrup and sugar in a stainless steel pot. Bring the mixture to a boil without stirring so that sugar will not crystallize on the sides of the pot. You may find it necessary to wash down the sides with a pastry brush and water. Boil sugar until it reaches 238 degrees on a candy thermometer.

Meanwhile, beat the egg yolks in an electric mixer until they are pale yellow. Once the syrup has reached the desired temperature, pour it slowly and carefully onto the egg yolks, mixing all the while and continue to beat the mixture for about 10 minutes to form a thick cream. Add the remaining cassis and the blackcurrants and refrigerate until chilled.

Beat chilled heavy cream in a cold bowl until it forms semi-stiff peaks. Fold whipped cream into the cassis cream. Line the inside of 6 or 8 wine glasses with soaked lady fingers, standing them up vertically. Pour in the mousse and freeze overnight. Place in the refrigerator for about 15 or 20 minutes before serving.

Sweet Seasons

The original Sweet Seasons was started in 1974 by three enterprising young people who had a dream of owning their own restaurant and a shoestring budget, but no formal restaurant management training. The realization of their dream was a tiny ten-table restaurant which they opened in the old railway depot on Wellfleet's Commercial Street, and here they were able to learn the restaurant business from the bottom up. Their restaurant soon became popular with people who appreciated fine food prepared by a kitchen which obviously enjoyed experimenting and trying out new ideas.

After three years at the Depot, the owners—Anne Fortier, Judith Pihl and Robert Morrill—were ready to expand and took over the spacious dining room at the Inn at Duck Creeke. The move to this beautiful old country inn proved to be so successful that when the property came up for sale, the partners decided they were ready for a permanent home and so purchased the inn, thereby becoming inn-keepers as well as restaurateurs.

The Inn at Duck Creeke is a five-acre complex in a delightful woodland setting that provides a sanctuary for many birds and species of wildlife. The many-windowed dining room overlooks the duck pond, where a pet flock of white Pekin ducks are now beginning to be joined by wild ducks returning to their old home. The entrance to the restaurant is down a flagstone path shaded by locust trees and bordered by colorful annuals. The restaurant has a summery feeling to it—it's light and airy, and a color scheme in the white/cream/yellow/green range accents polished wood tables and dark wood floors. Flowers on the tables, picked from the Inn's flower garden, and plenty of hanging plants add to the effect. Walls are decorated with lithographs and paintings from Wellfleet's art galleries, the most striking being the colorful silkscreen prints by local artist Judith Shahn, and all are for sale. A cocktail porch, furnished with antique white wicker, is a delightful place for an after-dinner drink, and leading off this porch is a tiny private dining room which is available for groups of 10 or 12 people. Live music, often a classical violin and guitar duet, accompanies dinner. Upstairs in the Tavern, where the atmosphere is more informal, there is nightly entertainment until midnight; here, lunch and dinner are served every day, while dinner only is served in the restaurant, except for brunch on weekends.

The food at Sweet Seasons is prepared with a light touch and is highly imaginative, though the menu contains traditional as well as unusual dishes. These range from such favorites as Scallops broiled in butter, garlic, herbs and wine, Swordfish with Lemon Butter or Bearnaise Sauce, Lobster poached in a court bouillon, and Steak Bearnaise, to such creations as Chicken Flamboyant (boneless breast of chicken on a bed of spinach and ham puree with hollandaise sauce), Steak au Poivre en Chemise (tenderloin wrapped in an herbed crepe and glazed with a brandy butter sauce), and Tropical Seafood & Melon Brochette in a Sambucca Marinade (see following recipe). Appetizers include Lobster-stuffed Artichoke bottoms, Chilled Marinated Shrimp, Wellfleet Oysters prepared in a variety of ways, and homemade soups—Lobster Bisque, Bloody Mary Soup (chilled gazpacho laced with vodka) and Chilled Strawberry Soup (see following recipe). Sweet Seasons' weekend brunch is extremely popular—they serve unusual egg dishes, omelettes, New Orleans French toast, fruited pancakes and salad plates.

Judy and Annie are the head chefs and are dedicated to the quality and attractive presentation of an interesting and creative menu, served in a pleasant atmosphere by a staff proud and happy to be a part of Sweet Seasons. They feel that because their staff returns to them every summer, a feeling of pride in the restaurant and a harmonious atmosphere is created that is evident throughout the business. This atmosphere, combined with the lovely setting and delicious food, makes dining at Sweet Seasons a unique experience.

Sweet Seasons at the Inn at Duck Creeke
East Main Street
Wellfleet, Mass. 02667
Telephone: 349-6535

Open: May through October; open seven days a week
　　　　from June 24 until Labor Day
Dinner: 6 to 10
Brunch: 10 to 2, weekends only
Children's portions: not available
License: full liquor license
Credit cards: AMEX, MC, VISA
Parking: ample private parking
Reservations: advised, call 349-6535

Chilled Strawberry Soup

Serves 10—12

3 pints strawberries
½ cup sugar
2 cups Burgundy
¼ cup flour
2 cups orange juice
1 cup water
3 cups sour cream
1 cup milk or light cream

Wash, hull and quarter strawberries. Cook in one cup of water for 10 minutes. Combine sugar and flour in a separate saucepan. Stir in the wine and orange juice. Stir or whisk constantly until mixture boils (approximately 10 minutes). Add to strawberries. Cool.

Puree in blender and add 3 cups of sour cream and one cup of milk or light cream. Chill. Served garnished with sliced strawberry and mint leaf.

Seasons Shrimp

Serves 4

4 large shrimp per person
2 large tomatoes, chopped coarsely
1 green pepper, thinly sliced
1 tablespoon chopped fresh parsley
½ teaspoon freshly-ground black pepper
1 clove garlic, minced
½ cup feta cheese, crumbled
1 or 2 ounces Ouzo
2 tablespoons butter
1 tablespoon olive oil

Saute the chopped tomatoes and peppers in olive oil and garlic for one minute. Add the peeled shrimp. Cook gently, keeping the pan moving during cooking. Add the freshly-ground black pepper. Pour Ouzo over the shrimp and flame. When flame subsides, remove shrimp to platter and arrange them with tails up. Sprinkle with crumbled feta cheese.

Heat sauce through and pour over the shrimp so cheese melts. Sprinkle with parsley and garnish with lemon wedges.

Poached Haddock with Leeks & Mussels   Serves 6

2 lbs. haddock or cod
4 dozen mussels
1 cup dry white wine
1 cup water (reserved from cooking vegetables)
½ cup leeks or scallions, finely sliced
½ cup heavy cream
¼ cup butter
¼ teaspoon nutmeg
2 tablespoons fresh chopped parsley
Salt and pepper to taste
½ cup each celery, carrots and zucchini
    cut in fine julienne, 1½" by ¼"

Cook julienne vegetables until tender but still firm. Reserve 1 cup of the cooking liquid to poach fish. Portion fish. Scrub and de-beard mussels. Bring water, wine and chopped leeks or scallions to a simmer. Add mussels, cover and steam for 5 minutes until they have opened. Remove mussels from their shells. Save some shells for garnish.

Strain liquid into a large skillet and add fish. Cover and gently simmer for 8 or 10 minutes until fish is flakey. Transfer fish to an oven-proof casserole and keep warm

Reduce liquid quickly to ½ cup. Add cream, seasonings and butter in small pieces, whisking constantly. Add the mussels and parsley and heat through. Pour sauce over fish. Top with julienne of carrots, celery and zucchini, and garnish with mussel shells.

Tropical Seafood & Melon Brochette

1 swordfish steak per person
Scallops and shrimp
Honeydew and canteloupe melon balls
Papaya, cut in chunks
Green pepper, cut in chunks

Marinade:

8 oz. butter
1 cup scallions, finely chopped
Juice of one lemon and one lime
1 tablespoon fresh chopped parsley

1 teaspoon each chopped marjoram, oregano, basil,
   thyme, garlic, ground nutmeg and black pepper
¼ cup Sambucca (or Ouzo or Pernod)

Melt butter in a heavy pan. Remove from heat and stir in marinade ingredients. Let sit while assembling brochettes.

Use wooden skewers—soak them in water first to prevent burning during cooking. Place seafood in a glass or ceramic bowl and cover with marinade. Marinate for at least one hour before cooking.

To assemble brochettes, alternate marinated seafood with melon balls, papaya and pepper pieces. Baste brochettes with marinade and broil or barbecue. Fish will be done when firm but tender.

Chilled Poached Lobster with Caviar Mayonnaise

Caviar mayonnaise:
2 eggs
3 tablespoons vinegar
⅔ teaspoon salt
½ teaspoon white pepper
2 teaspoons Dijon mustard
2 cups oil
2—4 tablespoons lemon juice
2 tablespoons boiling water
Small jar red caviar

Put all of the ingredients, except 1½ cups of oil, juice and water, in a blender. Blend at medium speed. Continue to blend while adding the rest of the oil in a slow steady stream. Add lemon juice to taste. Check seasoning. Blend in water. Chill for at least two hours, then fold in 3 teaspoons of red caviar before serving.

To poach a tender lobster: In a pot large enough to accommodate the number of lobsters to be cooked, place one inch of water, 1 or 2 bay leaves, 1 teaspoon peppercorns and two tablespoons of white wine or clam juice. Cover the pot and bring liquid to a slow simmer. Put lobsters into pot and cover. Cook for 15 minutes. Remove and refrigerate until chilled.

To serve: Remove claws from lobsters and crack with a cleaver. Twist tail from body. Cut tail lengthwise in shell with kitchen shears. Pick meat from body cavity and add to mayonnaise. Place lettuce leaves in body cavity and fill with caviar mayonnaise. Place lobsters and their claws on a platter covered with lettuce leaves. Garnish with black olives, parsley and wedges of lemon and hard boiled eggs.

Sautee of Calf's Liver Italienne

This dish is also excellent when veal is used instead of liver.

5 oz. calf's liver per person
4 tablespoons flour
½ teaspoon mace, nutmeg and pepper
2 tablespoons butter
1 tablespoon oil
1 large onion, thinly sliced
½ cup sliced mushrooms
2 tablespoons butter
½ cup white wine
1 tablespoon tomato paste
½ cup chicken stock
½ cup thinly-sliced and julienned ham
3 tablespoons chopped parsley
1 teaspoon tarragon

Melt two tablespoons of butter in a saucepan and add the onions. Cook gently until soft. Add mushrooms, increase heat and cook for about 4 minutes. Add the wine and boil to reduce liquid a little. Stir in tomato paste and stock. Cover and cook for about 10 minutes. Add the ham and warm through. Add the parsley, tarragon and pepper, stir and set aside in a warm place.

Sift flour with mace, nutmeg, salt and pepper. Coat liver with seasoned flour. Melt butter and oil in a skillet. Saute liver quickly for three minutes on each side until it is lightly browned. Shake pan frequently to prevent sticking. Arrange liver on a warm platter and cover with ham and mushroom mixture.

Towering Peach Almond Torte

Cake ingredients:
½ lb. butter at room temperature
1 cup sugar
8 egg yolks
2 teaspoons vanilla extract
2½ cups flour
1 teaspoon salt
1 tablespoon baking powder

¾ **cup milk**
3 **tablespoons dark rum**

9 **egg whites**
½ **teaspoon cream of tarter**
2¼ **cups sugar**
1 **cup sliced almonds**

Filling:

2 **cups heavy cream**
2 **tablespoons dark rum**
½ **cup confectioners sugar**
Sliced, peeled fresh peaches or other fresh fruit

Three 10" spring-form pans, greased and floured

Preheat oven to 350 degrees. Beat egg yolks and 1 cup of sugar to the ribbon stage. Beat in softened butter and vanilla.

Sift flour, baking powder and salt together. Mix rum with milk. Alternately add dry and liquid ingredients to egg yolk mixture, beating constantly. Spread each spring-form pan with ⅓ of the batter.

Beat egg whites until they foam. Add ½ teaspoon cream of tarter. Add 2¼ cups of sugar gradually and continue beating until the whites are stiff and glossy. Spread ⅓ of the meringue mixture over the batter in each pan and sprinkle with sliced almonds. Bake for 30 minutes at 350 degrees.

Carefully remove cakes from pans and place on a rack. Whip cream and flavor with confectioners sugar and rum. Reserve some whipped cream to decorate the top layer of the torte. Arrange fresh fruit on two layers and cover with remaining whippped cream. Stack the three layers one on top of the other and decorate the top layer with piped rosettes of reserved whipped cream.

Iced Mocha Espresso

Prepare strong espresso and chill in refrigerator. Fill a large (16 oz.) goblet or tall iced tea glass with small ice cubes.

Add: **2 oz. chilled espresso, 2 oz. heavy cream, 1 oz. Kahlua and 1 oz. Creme de Cocoa.** Stir to mix. Top glass with whipped cream and decorate with a twist of lemon peel and a whole coffee bean or a shake of cinnamon.

Toni-Lee's

Toni-Lee's restaurant in Hyannis successfully puts into practice a daring concept in dining out—in this single-menu restaurant with a seating capacity of 23, Toni-Lee's guests are seated at the same time and are served together, the components of the meal having been determined and prepared by Toni-Lee Caposella, the chef-owner.

With a Ph.D. in eighteenth century English literature, Toni-Lee spent four years teaching at college level before joining her husband, Dom Caposella, in establishing and managing their restaurant, Dom's, in Boston. Dom subsequently opened a restaurant in Hyannis for which Toni-Lee now acts as food consultant.

Toni-Lee opened her own restaurant in 1979 and this extract, written by her and taken from the introductory remarks on her menu, reads: "I decided to dispense with the traditional choice-of-menu format in my restaurant because I want to serve all my guests a meal which has been put together as an aesthetic and culinary whole. Menu planning involves much more than cooking well, although skill in the kitchen must be the cornerstone of any fine meal. Through cooking, eating, planning, traveling, reading, and thinking about food, one eventually learns how to establish a rhythm in the meal which makes every part interesting and delicious, but which also leaves a memorable and harmonious impression when the meal is done.

"There are different rhythms for different cuisines, and my preference is for discriminating eclecticism. I like to select from all the ethnic and regional patterns I have explored and enjoyed in my kitchen and my library. My repertoire currently includes French, Italian, Indian, Spanish, American, Chinese, Russian, and Mexican dishes."

Whatever the ethnic origins of the evening's meal might be, all ingredients consist of high-grade fresh foodstuffs, and the vegetables, fruits, fish and meats are fresh—not frozen, freeze-fried or extruded; local produce is used whenever possible. The dining room has purposefully been limited in size to permit the staff to prepare the food by hand, which includes beating eggs, whipping cream, rolling pastry and chopping vegetables. Toni-Lee plans the menu, purchases the food and cooks the meal, though her children sometimes help her wait on the guests.

The meals are all fixed price, usually $25 or $30, depending on the menu, and include appetizer, pasta or soup, main course, salad, cheese and fruit, dessert and cafe filtre or brewed tea (plus tax and service charge). Only fresh herbs and spices are used so that they impart their true flavors to sauces and dressings; salads are made with the crispest seasonal greens and dressed with olive oil and lemon; all the pasta is homemade and cooked *al dente*; unusual, carefully-chosen cheeses are complemented by perfectly-ripened fruit; and the coffee is a freshly-roasted blend of French roast and Mocha-Java beans, while the tea is loose Earl Gray.

Toni-Lee's is located one block east of the West End Rotary in Hyannis—the restaurant is informal and the decor understated to direct attention to the food. Dinner is served at 7:30 p.m. Wednesday through Saturday, year round. Seating is by reservation only—reservations are taken up to 3 p.m. for the same evening. Guests are required to give a credit card number when making a reservation; cancellations will be accepted until 5 p.m., but if guests do not cancel and do not show, the management reserves the right to charge for the cost of the food because of the personalized nature of the food preparation and the small capacity of the dining room.

Toni-Lee believes that by properly orchestrating a meal and choosing the right components, the whole can be greater than the sum of its parts. Certainly, this philosophy creates a dining experience that is unique, satisfying, and, on top of that, remarkably good value.

Toni-Lee's
645 Main Street
Hyannis, Mass. 02601
Telephone: 771-7340

Open: Wednesday through Saturday
Dinner: 7:30 p.m. seating only
Seats: 23
Children's portions: not available
License: Beer & Wine
Credit cards: MC, VISA, AMEX
Parking: on street parking only
Reservations: necessary, call 771-7340 before 3 p.m. for that evening.

Cold Cream of
Chicken Soup Senegalese

Serves 10

6 tablespoons butter
½ cup chopped onion
½ cup chopped leek
¼ cup chopped carrot
¼ cup chopped celery
1 medium apple, peeled, cored and chopped
2 tablespoons flour
2 tablespoons curry powder, warmed in oven
6 cups chicken stock, boiling
3 egg yolks
1 cup heavy cream
½ teaspoon lemon juice
Salt
1 cup julienned cooked chicken breast meat

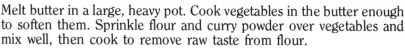

Melt butter in a large, heavy pot. Cook vegetables in the butter enough to soften them. Sprinkle flour and curry powder over vegetables and mix well, then cook to remove raw taste from flour.

Remove from heat and add boiling chicken stock, stirring well as you add it. Simmer soup for 1 hour.

Strain soup. Mix cream and egg yolks and stir in to the soup. Bring soup almost to a simmer, stirring. Season to taste, then chill thoroughly, preferably overnight.

To serve, place a tablespoon of julienned white chicken meat into each soup bowl or cup, then pour on soup. Garnish with chopped parsley or chopped scallions.

Blini

Serves 8

1 tablespoon yeast
1 cup milk
1 cup white flour
½ cup buckwheat flour
3 egg yolks and 3 egg whites,
	separated

½ teaspoon salt
¼ teaspoon sugar
3 tablespoons oil
3 tablespoons soured cream

Proof yeast in ½ cup warm water. Pour into a food processor and add all other ingredients except the egg whites. Mix well. Allow to rise in a warm place for about 2 hours, or until the mixture is bubbly and has risen.

Just before making the pancakes, whip egg whites with a pinch of salt and fold into the batter.

Cook pancakes on a griddle or in a frying pan coated with vegetable oil. Keep in a warm oven until ready to serve.

To serve, drizzle clarified butter over each pancake, place a mound of soured cream in the middle and a little red and black caviar on each side of it (a small jar of caviar goes a long way). Garnish with chopped scallions.

Pot de Creme

Serves 6 or 7

2 cups medium cream (not light)
1 heaping cup (6 or 7 oz.) grated chocolate
6 egg yolks
Liqueur to taste
Shaved chocolate and whipped cream for garnish

Melt 1 cup grated chocolate in the cream. Mix egg yolks. Pour chocolate and cream mixture over the egg yolks and stir gently until blended. Return to heat and cook until mixture begins to thicken.

Pour into small cups. Chill thoroughly. When chilled, pipe on whipped cream flavored with liqueur (Kahlua, Grand Marnier, Amaretto, etc.) and sprinkle with shaved chocolate (or use praline if you have added Amaretto to the whipped cream).

Restaurant Locations:

1. THE ARBOR
Route 28 at Route 6A
Orleans. 255-4847. Page 6.
Open all year/Lunch/Dinner/Bar.

2. CAFE ELIZABETH
31 Sea Street, Harwich Port
432-1147. Page 10.
Open all year/Dinner/Brunch.

3. CHANTERELLE
411 Main St., Yarmouthport
362-8195. Page 15.
Open all year/Lunch/Dinner.

4. CIELO
East Main Street, Wellfleet
349-2108. Page 20.
Seasonal/Lunch/Dinner (by reservation only)

5. CRANBERRY MOOSE
43 Main St., Yarmouthport
362-3501. Page 26
Open all year/Dinner.

6. DOM'S
337 Main St., Hyannis
771-6213. Page 31.
Open all year/Dinner.

7. IMPUDENT OYSTER
15 Chatham Bars Ave., Chatham
945-3545. Page 35.
Open all year/Lunch/Dinner/Bar

8. LA GRANDE RUE
551 Main St., Harwichport
432-1306. Page 40.
Open year round/Lunch/Dinner/Bar.

9. OLD MANSE INN
1861 Main St., Brewster
896-3149. Page 45.
Open most of the year/Dinner (by reservation only).

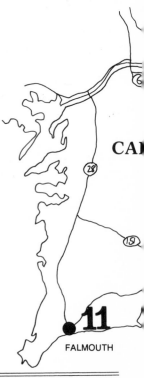

FALMOUTH

MAP

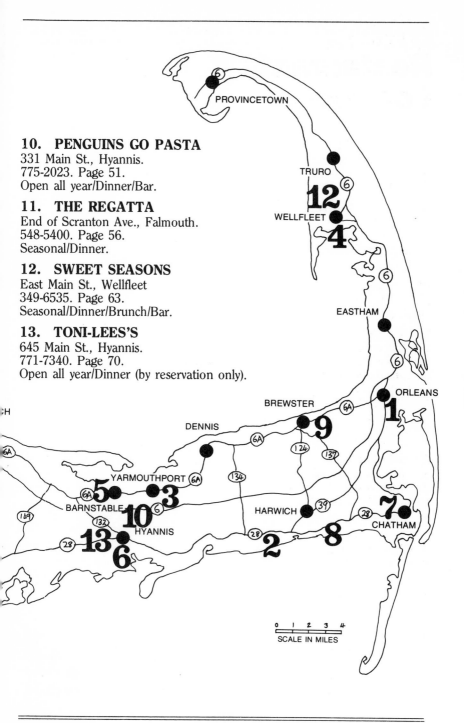

10. PENGUINS GO PASTA
331 Main St., Hyannis.
775-2023. Page 51.
Open all year/Dinner/Bar.

11. THE REGATTA
End of Scranton Ave., Falmouth.
548-5400. Page 56.
Seasonal/Dinner.

12. SWEET SEASONS
East Main St., Wellfleet
349-6535. Page 63.
Seasonal/Dinner/Brunch/Bar.

13. TONI-LEES'S
645 Main St., Hyannis.
771-7340. Page 70.
Open all year/Dinner (by reservation only).

Index